ADVENT REFLECTIONS

ADVENT REFLECTIONS

Meditations for a Holy Advent

EDITED BY BRANDON MCGINLEY

EWTN PUBLISHING, INC.
IRONDALE, ALABAMA

Cover design by LUCAS Art & Design, Jenison, MI.

On the cover: by Guido Reni
(1575–1642), oil on canvas, 1640, © IanDagnall
Computing / Alamy Stock Photo (G29XR6).

EWTN Publishing, Inc.
5817 Old Leeds Road, Irondale, AL 35210

Distributed by Sophia Institute Press, Box 5284, Manchester, NH 03108.

Library of Congress Cataloging-in-Publication Data

Names: McGinley, Brandon, editor. | Eternal Word Television Network.
Title: Advent reflections : meditations for a holy Advent.
Description: Irondale, Alabama : EWTN Publishing, Inc., 2019. Summary:
   "Reflections from bishops and priests for each week of Advent"—
   Provided by publisher.
Identifiers: LCCN 2019042663 ISBN 9781682781074 (paperback) ISBN
   9781682781081 (ebook)
Subjects: LCSH: Advent—Meditations.
Classification: LCC BX2170.A4 A39 2019 DDC 242/.332—dc23
LC record available at https://lccn.loc.gov/2019042663

First printing

CONTENTS

First Week of Advent

Second Week of Advent

Third Week of Advent

Fourth Week of Advent

Christmas

ADVENT REFLECTIONS

FIRST WEEK OF ADVENT

WATCHFUL WAITING

Archbishop Michael Neary, 2004

Ballintubber Abbey, County Mayo, Ireland

‿‿

The Gospel reading for this Sunday,[1] the First Sunday of Advent and the first Sunday of the Church's liturgical year, comes from St. Matthew. And central to Matthew's Gospel are the Person of Jesus Christ, discipleship, and the Church.

In presenting Jesus, Matthew is eager to underline the continuity between Jesus and the Old Testament. Jesus is the fulfillment of the hopes and longings of the people of the Old Covenant. Indeed, this Gospel was probably written specifically with Jewish Christians in mind—early converts from Judaism whom Matthew wanted to reassure that Christ

[1] Lectionary Cycle C.

fulfilled everything they had looked forward to, everything they had hoped would be brought to fulfillment. Predictably, then, Matthew makes copious use of the Old Testament, more so than any other evangelist. Matthew frequently presents Jesus as a new Moses, One Who fulfills the law.

And so, Matthew is aware of the hopes and the longings of the Jewish people — which at times were quite narrow and nationalistic, even neurotically so — but at the same time, he is also concerned about demonstrating the universality of the Christian Gospel. The message is for the whole world. The risen Christ at the end of St. Matthew's Gospel gives a mandate: "Go therefore and make disciples of all nations" (28:19).

One of the great tensions in the early Church centered precisely on this question of narrow nationalism on the one hand and the universalism — the catholicity — of the Christian Gospel on the other. The evangelist emphasizes that what is important is not belonging to a particular race but rather, being open to God's grace. In keeping with this idea, we find that in this Gospel, the outsiders — that is, non-Jews — respond more wholeheartedly in faith to Jesus than do the insiders. This is why Matthew focuses on people such as the Magi, the centurions, and the Syro-Phoenician woman.

Matthew also likes to present Jesus as a great healer and a great teacher, especially in that He comes to fulfill the law. We see this very much in the Sermon on the Mount, where Christ teaches that it is in reconciliation and love that we fulfill the demands and the purpose of the law. Matthew also stresses the consistency in the life of Jesus, in what He does and what He teaches. This relationship between teaching and doing is central to Christ's message and to Matthew's interest in forming disciples.

The disciple is not one who just says, "Lord, Lord," but rather one who carries out the Will of the Father (Matt. 7:21–23). By contrast, the leaders of Israel at the time taught, but they did not put their teaching into practice. Jesus highlights the hypocrisy of the Pharisees as a warning for Christians: This is the pitfall that awaits those whose actions do not correspond with their words.

Judgment and responsibility, therefore, are other central themes in Matthew's Gospel. We find these coming through in so many of Christ's parables: the faithful steward (24:45–51), the wise and foolish virgins (25:1–13), the talents (25:14–30), and the sheep and the goats (25:31–46).

As for presenting the disciples, Matthew is much more compassionate than Mark, who could be quite hard on them. Matthew recognizes discipleship as a mixture of faith and fear. We can see this in chapter 14, when Jesus invites Peter to come to Him across the water. First, Peter steps out in faith, but then he becomes conscious of the stormy seas, takes his eye off Jesus Christ, and begins to lose faith and to sink. Matthew is very concerned about the Church and Her leaders, giving us an insight into the true spirit and values that ought to prevail in the Church: reconciliation, forgiveness, and compassion.

Now, in the first chapter of the Gospel of Matthew, Jesus is known by the name "Emmanuel." The evangelist is very conscious of the covenant God made with His people, and "Emmanuel" means, "God with us." And then, at the end of St. Matthew's Gospel, we find the Great Commission:

> Go therefore and make disciples of all nations, baptizing them in the name of the Father and of the Son and of the Holy Spirit, teaching them to observe all that I have commanded you; and lo, I am with you always, to the close of the age. (28:19–20)

Notice, again, the reminder that God is with us. The life of Jesus bridges "Emmanuel," meaning God with *His people* and meaning God with *the whole world.*

The early Church was nearly torn asunder by factions forming around tensions between the new and the old.

Thus, we can see Matthew not throwing away Jewish tradition, but rather interpreting it in the light of Jesus Christ, Who brings it to fulfillment. He is writing to emphasize the continuity between the Old and New Covenants; he is articulating a comprehensive whole. You'll notice that when Matthew is quoting the Old Testament, he frequently uses a formula: "this was to fulfill what was spoken by the Lord through the prophets" (see, for example, 1:22 and 2:17) Therefore, the old traditions take up a new meaning with St. Matthew. This Gospel, therefore, has a particular relevance for us today as we address, once again, a sense of rupture from the past.

Now, during the Advent season, the Church is alert, watching, and waiting. In today's Gospel, Jesus encourages us to stay awake, to stand ready. Advent has a twofold character: On the one hand, it is a season when we are preparing to remember Christ's birthday, trying to situate ourselves among those who lived before the time of Jesus Christ and looked forward to His coming; on the other hand, Advent directs our minds and hearts, here and now, to preparing for Christ's second coming. We are living between two Advents, between two comings of Christ—His coming at Christmas in the Incarnation, and His final coming at the end of time.

In the Church of St. Matthew's time, there was uninformed enthusiasm about the end time. Matthew acknowledges and addresses this situation, making clear that the end is not yet. Every generation needs to relearn that lesson and apply it to its own situation. Matthew stresses, however, that we must also not fall into apathy. This is why today's Gospel wants to instill a sense of urgency, a sense of appropriate vigilance. Matthew wants our preparation to have a moral dimension: The end may come at any time, so we must be prepared to give an account to the Lord.

In this Gospel (Matt. 24:37–44), Matthew takes up the idea that the end time will, in many respects, resemble the time at the beginning. And so we have the mention of Noah and the flood, which was a judgment on the world that anticipated the final judgment. The flood came as people were going about their ordinary daily chores; given our lack of knowledge about the end time, a leisurely approach to repentance would be foolish. Fear of being caught off guard ought to motivate our alertness.

We are an impatient generation. In our technological age, light comes with the flip of a switch, water with the turn of a tap, food with the opening of the refrigerator door. Communication from one end of the world to the other takes only an instant. We are conditioned by all of this.

In a world that is geared toward immediate fulfillment of everyday desires, it can be difficult to look to the future, to look to the end. But this is what St. Matthew is encouraging us to do in today's Gospel. It is only looking to the end that will enable us to understand the meaning of the present.

Jesus, through Matthew, is asking us to see through the present to what is to come. One way of undertaking this preparation is to listen to the Lord, as the prophet Isaiah reminds us in the first reading (Isa. 2:1–5), "that he may teach us his ways and that we may walk in his paths."

We can also notice that in the Second Reading (Rom. 13:11–14), there is an emphasis on the fact that we do not know the time of judgment. We must wake up now. Paul tells the Christians in Rome to avoid sin in preparation for the coming of the end time: "Let us conduct ourselves becomingly as in the day, not in reveling and drunkenness, not in debauchery and licentiousness, not in quarreling and jealousy." When people are engaged full time in satisfying their own cravings, they are not disposed to face reality or the future — and they are not disposed to take responsibility in the present.

Jesus talks about the return of the Son of Man in order to encourage us to be responsible in the present, because fidelity in the present is the best preparation for the future.

THE IN-BETWEEN TIME

Bishop Alan Hopes, 2005

St. Etheldreda Church, Ely Place, London, England

Already we are sensing a gathering momentum as Christmas approaches. There are gifts to be carefully chosen, cards to be written and mailed, office parties and family gatherings to attend — and, of course, the vital preparations for Christmas itself, decorations, and trees and meals, and so on. I do hope you enjoy all of these activities! Christmas is certainly about rejoicing, and a lot of hard work has to go into preparing a good celebration.

And so we are caught up over the next few weeks in the unreality of both celebrating and preparing for Christmas — as if we are preparing to celebrate something we are already celebrating. But that is actually a very good description of Advent: We are preparing to celebrate the coming of the Lord, which has already taken place at the Nativity *and* is still to happen at the end of time. The Lord *has come* and the Lord *is coming* to save us. That is the lens through which we need to see the readings of Advent.

Let's first pause and ask ourselves what it means to be "saved." What is the Lord saving us from? What is He saving us for? Whom, precisely, is He saving? To "save" someone suggests that someone is in some kind of danger or captivity. From the perspective of eternity, that is certainly true of the human race: Since the Fall of Adam, we have been held captive by the devil and his wiles. Evil seeks to ensnare us in subtle, devious ways because it is so unlovely that no one could possibly be naturally attracted to it. In the same way, the devil tried to deceive God Himself—but God outwitted him. And so God Himself enters the story to set free the creatures He created and loves. That is why He left the glory of Heaven to come down to earth at Christmas.

Sadly, of course, we remain trapped by our willfulness and ignorance. We have learned well too many lessons from the Fall—lessons of selfishness, of self-importance, of deviousness. We continue to be filled with pride, with covetousness, with lust and envy, with anger, gluttony, and sloth. But God comes to save us from all this as well!

We can turn, then, to the question "What are we saved for?" Here we see that Jesus comes to save us for eternal happiness and bliss with Him, not only in Heaven but also in this life. For salvation is not an abstract concept but a concrete reality. When we cooperate with God, He saves us from evil and from its consequences—from sin, from everlasting death, and from ourselves. This is not only for the future in Heaven, but also for here and now. Happiness—true, lasting contentment—is a possibility when we live in accord with God's Will for our lives.

Finally, we consider "Whom, precisely, is God saving?" We are, of course, saved as individuals: Each one of us has a story and a special place in God's heart. But we must beware of making ourselves the center of the story, because we are part of a community, a body. When God enters into a covenant with His people, it is with the whole of the people, not just with individuals in it. He made His first salvation covenant with the people of Israel, and His New Covenant with His Bride, the Church.

This communal aspect is a key part of the Catholic understanding of salvation, and if we miss it, we end up placing ourselves at the center of the universe, just like the secular culture around us, which is precisely what God is trying to save us from! We can see this clearly at Mass when we receive Holy Communion as individuals but also as part of the community of the faithful. At the words of Consecration, we hear that the Lord is saving each one of us as part of His people—saving us from the devil, from sin, from death, and from ourselves, saving us for the glory of Heaven and for happiness on earth.

Let us turn to the readings for this First Sunday of Advent and see how they help us to prepare for this great act of salvation.[2] There are three figures who are central to the Advent readings and who will help us in this time of preparation. The first is the great prophet Isaiah, who foretells the coming of the Savior; the second is John the Baptist, who proclaims the arrival of the Savior; and, of course, the third is Mary who gives birth to the Promised One of Israel. We begin, appropriately in the First Reading of the first week of the season, with Isaiah (63:16b–17, 19b; 64:2–7).

The prophet Isaiah lived in Judah in the eighth century before Christ, about a century in advance of the nation's destruction by Nebuchadnezzar of Babylon. Isaiah addresses himself to a demoralized people at the end of their greatness, a people who bemoan their lost days of empire and

[2] Lectionary Cycle B.

who look wistfully back on the glittering days of King David and King Solomon.

Isaiah will have none of that nostalgia. "Look at yourselves," he says in effect, "not at your fantasies about the past. Look at your own moral condition now!" He speaks of those who accumulate vast private fortunes at the expense of others; of the needs and rights of the poor, the disadvantaged, the unemployed; and of the abuse of power and the absence of real justice in the social structures of his nation. "How can the people of Judah worship God," he asks, "when their lives are so complacent when it comes to upholding God's values and so active when it comes to acquiring money and prestige?" Isaiah is rightfully majestic in his condemnation: "We all fade like a leaf, and our iniquities, like the wind, take us away" (Isa. 64:6).

What Isaiah said to the people of his own day is equally applicable to us and to future generations. We must be spiritually prepared for the coming of Jesus by living lives of integrity — by allowing God's values and God's justice to reign in our hearts and to guide our lives, not just here and there but through and through, as we make our pilgrim journey toward Him.

THE PROMISE OF LIGHT

Fr. Ronald Creighton-Jobe, 2006

Little Oratory, London, England

One of the great themes of Advent is the contrast between darkness and light as symbols of the hope at the heart of the Christian message. Darkness and light return time and time again in the Scriptures, starting at the very beginning: God gives light to the dark nothingness that preceded Creation. That light is extended to us in a particular way in this season, as we await the light of Christ, which shines in a world that in many ways appears to be without hope.

We know, of course, that the world is never really without hope. Our faith gives us the confidence that the victory was won by Christ through His Incarnation, Death, and Resurrection. And the feast of the Nativity, which we are preparing for, is about that central message of hope. We cannot live without hope, and Advent, above all, is a time of hope, prayer, perseverance, and repentance.

Now, let's go back to that theme of creation. In Genesis, we see the image of God's breath wafting over the void and creating order and life. Recall in the Easter Vigil that great moment when the light of Christ enters the darkness of the church. And then, we know, a tragedy occurred. Man, who was the fullness of God's creation, His masterpiece, turned away from the light, turned away from all that God wishes him to be, and plunged himself into the darkness of sin.

Sin is also a theme that we turn to in Advent—not in despair but in thanksgiving for the gift of our Redeemer. Man's sinfulness, the darkness of our souls, receives the radiant light of Christ. Our world is hungering for that light, and so we must be messengers of that hope. Can you imagine what our first parents must have experienced when they left the radiance of the life in the Garden, thrust into a world into which they had brought sin and darkness by turning their backs on the light? We know the story: Pain, sorrow, suffering, and death itself all enter, and Cain kills Abel, the first of a long line of horror stories. Paganism, a world without God, is not attractive. It is darkness.

Primitive man was surrounded by fear. His whole life was determined by it. It was immensely important that the sun and the moon should rise, that all the forces of nature should function, that the rivers should overflow and recede. And so to make certain that these things would happen, the man-made gods had to be placated. This was done by the sacrifice of things that were precious — even human life.

The kings of these nations, as they were described in Scripture, were often the high priests of the pagan cults who exercised the power of life and death over their subjects. Human life counted for nothing against the value of keeping the gods placated. If you would ask a pagan about his relationship with the gods, he would not understand it except in terms of fear.

This is the context in which the Light of God came — darkness, hatred, envy, fear. "The people who walked in darkness have seen a great light; those who dwelt in a land of deep darkness, on them has light shined" (Isa. 9:2). It began with a man called Abram. He left everything that gave him security, and he went on a journey because he was convinced that the Living God had called him. At the heart of that call was a promise: "Look toward heaven, and number the stars, if you are able to number them.... So shall your descendants be" (Gen. 15:5).

And so Abram went into the desert—and this is our journey, too, because everything that occurs in Scripture has a message for each one of us. The journey into light —into God's gift of Himself in revelation—is a long one, and it is reflected in our own life journeys. However long we live, we will always seek light. Like Abram, now called Abraham, we are called by name. In our Baptism we are called to be children of the light.

God made a promise to Abraham, just as He does to us, and Abraham had to make an act of faith, just as we do, in response. Abraham's act of faith is, however, far more dramatic than anything we will likely face. God calls on him to sacrifice his only son—the sign of his immortality, the proof of God's love. And so, Abraham takes the knife in faith and trust. It seems to be an act against all hope, but no, it is an act of hope in God, and for this reason Abraham is our father in faith.

But God intervenes, and the light of His love shines forth in that statement of Abraham, "God will provide himself the lamb"—a substitute (Gen. 22:8). The sacrifice—the true and whole sacrifice—is fulfilled much later, but here we see the beginning of the concept that we are to make of ourselves a sacrifice, the gift of ourselves to a loving God—not to placate Him, but because we want to give ourselves to Him as He has given Himself to us.

By Moses' time, the covenant, the binding agreement between God and Abraham, seemed to have been dashed by the slavery in Egypt. But we know that that was not the end of the story. And so God opens up His inner life to Moses by giving His name, "I AM WHO I AM" (Exod. 3:14). God wants us not only to know things about Him but to enter into intimacy with Him. To know someone's name is to enter into a relationship with that person. The light of revelation is opened in God's communication of His very self to His people, and He delivers them through the Red Sea, a symbol of Baptism.

God also made it clear, though, that to be in relationship with Him implies responsibilities. Friendship must be reciprocal. And so we have Commandments, through which God shows us what it means to be in a responsible relationship with Him — not just to receive from Him, but to live maturely and to grow in love. The Commandments are not about simple prohibitions or coercion, but about teaching us how to respond to God in love.

Ultimately, that is the choice we are faced with. God gives us the gift of free will. We may say yes to Him, or we may say no to Him. But in our yes or no there are consequences, and this comes through especially in Advent. We are called to light. When we sin, when we fall again into darkness, we must remember that the light is always there for us in the form of the sacrament of Penance. Indeed, Advent's focus on repentance, on returning to and embracing Christ's light, is exactly why this sacrament is such an important part of our Advent observance.

Confession is a sacrament of hope, that great theme of Advent, and a sacrament of healing. Even when God's people turn their back on Him, He calls them back. How fortunate we are to have been given the means to turn from our darkness — and the darkness that surrounds us in the world — to the light of Christ through His forgiving grace.

Through revelation, we see how the light of God draws His people slowly but inexorably back to Himself. God never abandons His people. He loves them — that is, us. He creates us for communion out of that love. When we acknowledge our sinfulness, that darkness within us, we do so with the knowledge that "Christ has died, Christ is risen." The Incarnation is the very heart of God's revelation, and it is this that we are preparing for during these weeks.

We prepare by living the sacred liturgy as profoundly and as deeply as we possibly can. We prepare by living the wonderful readings the Church prescribes for this season of Advent, which resound more and more deeply in our hearts as we prepare for Christmas. Scripture tells us to have confidence, to believe, to persevere, and, above all, to be children of light.

As we think about this, we will know in our hearts that this message is what draws us into reality — not the world of nonsense and darkness in which we live — but the reality that has at its heart a Baby, a weak, humble Baby dependent on His Mother and yet the Creator of the World. What greater source of life can there be for each one of us than to know that God has become flesh and that He dwells among us? That is the mystery of Christmas for which we pray and hope in this season of Advent joy.

Death, Joy, and Living in Christ

Fr. Richard Biggerstaff, 2010

St. Anthony of Padua Church, Rye, England

The Church offers us two great seasons of preparation: Lent and Advent. But they are never just about preparation for a feast; rather, they are about preparing us for Heaven itself. We must not trick ourselves into thinking that all we need to do is look back; we must look forward and take stock of our progress and future in the business of holiness.

I'd like to highlight three Advent themes that have a particular resonance for me and that are part of the language of the Church in this season. The first of the Advent themes is death. But we must speak of the reality and the certainty of our inevitable death in the light of Advent hope.

Pope Benedict XVI, speaking at the beginning of Advent in 2007, said this: "Every year this basic spiritual attitude [of Advent hope] is reawakened in the hearts of Christians, who, while they prepare to celebrate the great Feast of Christ the Savior's Birth, revive the expectation of his glorious second coming at the end of time."[3] This is a good reminder in a season when we can easily get swept along by all the traditions of preparing for the feast—but those traditions must be accompanied by the deeper preparation for the fulfillment of the mysteries that Christmas proclaims. The coming of the Lord in our history looks forward to "his glorious return, so every personal existence is called to be measured against him—in a mysterious and multiform way—during the earthly pilgrimage, in order to be found 'in him' at the moment of his return."[4]

The second theme I'd like to highlight is our way of life—that is, the necessity of really living in Christ, not just being inspired by Him. Christ is not simply the Man of Galilee, Whom we follow; rather, His life lives in us, and the flourishing of His life in us becomes the means by which we flourish. His life and grace become the means

---

[3] Vespers homily, December 1, 2007.

[4] Vespers homily, November 26, 2005.

by which we can do heroic things for love. In sum, His life becomes the very definition of our lives so that we can truly be His, truly Christian.

The third theme is that of joy, the hallmark of a good companion. Joy is energizing and pure. It is true that these weeks fill many with dread — the dread of what it is to be alive. As Christmas approaches, there are so many in our communities who would prefer not to be around all these celebrations. There is the burden of depression, which is exacerbated by the darkness and the sometimes forced festiveness — that parody of joy that can become deeply unsatisfying.

In talking to the young people of Scotland in Glasgow, Pope Benedict put it like this:

> My dear young Catholics ... I urge you to lead lives worthy of our Lord (cf. Eph. 4:1) and of yourselves. There are many temptations placed before you every day ... which the world tells you will bring you happiness, yet these things are destructive and divisive. There is only one thing which lasts: the love of Jesus Christ personally for each one of you. Search for him, know him and love him, and he will set you free from slavery to the glittering but superficial

existence frequently proposed by today's society. Put aside what is worthless and learn of your own dignity as children of God.[5]

Now let us turn to the readings for the First Sunday of Advent,[6] which begin with a passage from Isaiah, who foreshadows the Birth of Jesus Christ — His Birth, His life, and indeed, His Resurrection. On the First Sunday of Advent, we hear the prophet speak in the voice of God and call the people of Israel to repentance in order to prepare for the coming of His Son (2:1–5). But the Old Testament people of Israel also represent the New Testament Church, so the call to repentance applies to us as well. Christ has already come, but His coming again at the end of time necessitates that we prepare our souls. We need to walk in the light of the Lord just as surely as the Israelites of Isaiah's time did.

At the heart of the message, we have the mysterious image of the mountain. "It shall come to pass in the latter days that the mountain of the house of the LORD shall be established as the highest of the mountains, and shall be raised above the hills; and all the nations shall flow to it."

[5] Eucharistic celebration, September 16, 2010.
[6] Lectionary Cycle A.

(Isa. 2:2). The idea of the mountain of God as the goal of all nations is a very ancient one. Isaiah, however, has a more precise image in mind: that of the mountain of the Temple of the Lord. This is the place of worship, but it is also the place where the unity of nations can be seen. It is the city of peace, Jerusalem.

Centuries later, Jesus will triumphantly enter Jerusalem to be crowned as King, and it is where the Word of God will spend His last days before His Crucifixion. Outside the city, His outstretched arms will draw all people to Him, and in the city, He will instruct His apostles to stay and to wait for the coming of the Holy Spirit, the promise of the Father. Through Jerusalem came salvation to the world. Through Jerusalem came the meaning of true love. Through Jerusalem came the fulfillment of everlasting justice and peace in the Kingdom of God. Thus, we can now truly say, "Let us walk in the light of the LORD!" (Isa. 2:5).

The Second Reading for this Sunday comes from the Letter to the Romans (13:11–14), in which we're reminded of the urgency of this present time. Salvation is even nearer to us now. We cannot halt time, and if we attempt to do so through a disordered nostalgia or by burdening ourselves with regrets, we halt the very business of life itself.

Rather, we are to look to the coming of the Lord and live in recognition of our God-given dignity. We live with the joy this hope brings.

These verses remind us of the importance of our daily decision for God. At the beatification of St. John Henry Newman, Pope Benedict spoke of Newman's motto, *Cor ad cor loquitur*, or "Heart speaks unto heart":

> [This motto] gives us an insight into his understanding of the Christian life as a call to holiness, experienced as the profound desire of the human heart to enter into intimate communion with the Heart of God. He reminds us that faithfulness to prayer gradually transforms us into the divine likeness.[7]

The Gospel of St. Matthew this week (24:37–44) also speaks of the return of Jesus, reminding us of the necessity of decisive watchfulness. Christ paints a picture of everyday normality in His words to His apostles, but it is precisely in the "normal" times that we are most likely to forget about Him. Everything feels the same as usual — boring, even — but the truth is that life is completely out of balance.

[7] Homily at the Beatification Mass for Cardinal John Henry Newman, September 19, 2010.

There is no room for God, because we have filled up that space with self—our worries and concerns and desires. There is no room for worship, because our relentless search for substitutes has left us exhausted and hardened. There is no room for charity, because we have distracted ourselves with endlessly complicated questions about our own time and resources, leaving us without answers and numb to the needs of others.

Pope Benedict said in an Advent address that "man is the one creature free to say 'yes' or 'no' to eternity, that is, to God."[8] A human being is able to extinguish hope within him by eliminating God from his life. How can it happen that the creature made for God, intimately oriented to Him, can deprive himself of this richness? God knows, however, that those who reject Him have not recognized His true face. And so He never ceases to knock on the door of our souls like a humble pilgrim in search of hospitality. Let us use this Advent season to respond to that knock.

After all, this is the beginning of a new liturgical year. It is a gift of God, Who wished to reveal Himself to us in the mystery of Christ through the world and through the sacraments. Pope Benedict concluded those Advent vespers

[8] Vespers homily, December 1, 2007.

with this beautiful prayer to Our Lady, a fitting conclusion to this reflection:

> O Mary, Virgin of expectation and Mother of hope, revive the spirit of Advent in your entire Church, so that all humanity may start out anew on the journey towards Bethlehem, from which it came, and that the Sun that dawns upon us from on high will come once again to visit us.

SECOND WEEK OF ADVENT

Transformational Hope

Archbishop Michael Neary, 2004

Ballintubber Abbey, County Mayo, Ireland

The readings on this Second Sunday of Advent[9] are shot through with the idea of hope, which is a public, shared yearning. What God has promised—and what God will give, should we accept His grace—is a foundational change in the nature of social relationships. Heralding this, we meet this week a rather strange figure: John the Baptist. John has a wilderness wardrobe and a desert diet. He is a tough-talking, uncompromising character. He preaches in the Palestinian desert, which goes on as far as the eye can see. This is a place where we are stripped of the luxuries

[9] Lectionary Cycle A.

of life—and also of many of its distractions. In the desert, people are more open to God and more receptive to His Word.

When we reflect on the history of the people of God, we notice that in the desert the people were vulnerable, and so they recognized their dependence on God and therefore were more faithful to Him. It was when the people became settled in the Promised Land that they became careless, depending on themselves more than on God. They began to take Him for granted; while they paid a great of attention to fulfilling the requirements of the liturgy and worship, their daily lives were defined by greed and exploitation. There was little concern for the weak and the poor, the marginalized and the vulnerable.

This settled community began to compromise the religious values and ideals that had sustained them for so long. They felt that God could be paid off in worship. And so, when the prophet Hosea was anxious to lead the people back to a proper relationship with the Lord, he invited them to come again into the desert, where he would speak to them as in their youth. It was in keeping with this idea that John the Baptist preached in the wilderness. His message is clear, concise, and consistent: "Repent, for the kingdom of heaven is at hand" (Matt. 3:2).

Now, this repentance is not simply emotional sorrow or regret for the past. Rather, it has a present and a future dimension: It involves a resolute turning away from sin and a wholehearted turning toward the Lord. It involves getting our hearts in the right place and then living accordingly.

This repentance can never be a merely human initiative. It is always God's grace to which we respond when we repent. And we repent because the Lord is at hand and the Kingdom of God is close by. John the Baptist proclaimed a God who cares, but also a God who demands accountability. Therefore, John challenged the privileged position that has been claimed by the Pharisees and the Sadducees.

John the Baptist called everyone to change their ways, and when he saw the Pharisees and the Sadducees coming, he was not overawed by them. He was not going to tailor his message to suit to leaders of the Jewish religion. The Pharisees were the people of the book who were familiar with the law; therefore, they were expected to know God's will as illustrated in the law. The Sadducees, on the other hand, were a priestly caste who conducted the liturgies in the Temple. John warned them that they would not be spared judgment simply because they belonged to the chosen people. They, too, must repent. John realized that people in the professional class were frequently more concerned about their status and ancestry than the fruits of their lives or the future of their souls. So, John confronted them about the precariousness of their situation: "Even now the axe is laid to the root of the trees; every tree therefore that does not bear good fruit is cut down and thrown into the fire" (Matt. 3:10). If they did not repent, John asserted, they would be judged by the One who comes after him. On this Second Sunday of Advent, John the Baptist's call for repentance is addressed to each one of us. We are called upon to listen to the Word of God and to put that Word into practice. In this way we prepare for the One Who is to come, for Jesus Christ Himself.

This Sunday's Gospel turns from threat to promise and then to hope: The One who is to come will baptize with the Holy Spirit and with fire, which is both frightening and exhilarating. As we look into our own hearts, then, we discover pockets of resistance; we discover areas in our lives that need to be changed and touched by God's forgiving power.

If we link this Sunday's Gospel with the readings that precede it, we will notice a very definite emphasis on hope: What God has promised and will bring about is a very definite change in social relationships. In the reading from the prophet Isaiah, the focus is on God's Spirit—His Life-Giving

Power — Who can create newness out of nothing. This creative Power is completely beyond our control, and the result of His intervention will be a wide-ranging transformation with implications for the whole world and even the animal kingdom: a restored, reconciled creation, in which brutality will be tamed and old enemies will become friends — the wolf and the lamb, the calf and the lion, the cow and the bear. In other words, the fragile and the vulnerable will be protected by God's intervention. This underlines the truth that what God offers is sheer gift — a gift that we, left to ourselves, could not achieve. It is pure grace.

And while we wait the Birth of the One who will bring this about, the Responsorial Psalm accentuates the fact that the King has a responsibility to establish justice throughout His domain. Honesty, gentleness, truth, and compassion will prevail because that is the very nature of this King. By building on the qualities that God brings to us in His gift, we can enter into new relationships with the Lord and with each other. We can become the means of the social transformation the Lord has promised, bringing the light and peace of the Christ Child to the world.

Threefold Advent

Bishop Alan Hopes, 2005

St. Etheldreda Church, Ely Place, London, England

The season of Advent has developed from a number of sources. In the churches of Gaul and Spain, it started as an ascetical season of penitence in preparation for Christmas, similar to Lent. In the Christian East, however, the development was very different. There, the Church remained deeply wounded by the Christological controversies of the fourth to sixth centuries — scarred by division over the divine and human natures of Jesus. Therefore, Advent in the Eastern rites became a time to affirm the orthodox faith regarding the Incarnation and the Person of Christ, a time to summon up the witness of the prophets and forerunners of the Savior so that they might bear witness to Him and sing His praises.

In Rome, the development was also different: The Church co-opted pagan practices. The pagan gods each had their own temple, and at a certain time each year, the god was said to make an appearance in its temple. A statue would be moved into a prominent position, and the temple was opened for celebration. This temple appearance was known as an *adventus*. In addition, in Rome, the anniversary of the accession of the emperor was celebrated each year as his *adventus*.

The Christmas feast is also related to the pagan celebration of the birthday (*dies natalis*) of the unvanquished sun of the winter solstice. As we celebrated the Nativity of the Lord, these pagan festivals were soon forgotten. But they had their influence: In the Roman Rite, the predominant emphasis became one of preparing for the past and the future coming of the Lord, based on the old rites of *adventus* and *dies natalis*.

These three sources of our season of Advent jostle for attention each year: in the focus on penitence and the need to seek forgiveness, the summoning of the heralds of the Good News to bear witness to the Redeemer, and the celebration of the past and the future coming of the Lord. In the readings for the Second Sunday of Advent,[10] all three of these elements appear.

[10] Lectionary Cycle B.

In the First Reading, Isaiah (40:1–5, 9–11) proclaims a great message of consolation, telling a conquered people of the triumphant return of the Lord their God—in effect, His *adventus*. And in the Gospel, John the Baptist appears in the wilderness as the witness who heralds the coming Messiah, and he makes this proclamation by calling the people to repentance. But let us concentrate for a moment on the element of the heralds of the Savior.

The vocations of Isaiah and John the Baptist are very much intertwined. Here are Isaiah's words in this Sunday's reading:

> Comfort, comfort my people, says your God. Speak tenderly to Jerusalem, and cry to her that her warfare is ended, that her iniquity is pardoned, that she has received from the LORD's hand double for all her sins. A voice cries: "In the wilderness prepare the way of the LORD, make straight in the desert a highway for our God. Every valley shall be lifted up, and every mountain and hill be made low; the uneven ground shall become level, and the rough places a plain. And the glory of the LORD shall be revealed, and all flesh shall see it together, for the mouth of the LORD has spoken." ...

Get you up to a high mountain, O Zion, herald of good tidings; lift up your voice with strength, O Jerusalem, herald of good tidings, lift it up, fear not; say to the cities of Judah, "Behold your God!" Behold, the Lord God comes with might, and his arm rules for him; behold, his reward is with him, and his recompense before him. He will feed his flock like a shepherd, he will gather the lambs in his arms, he will carry them in his bosom, and gently lead those that are with young.

Isaiah's prophecies are what we might call the remote preparation for the coming of Christ. He lived in the seventh century before Christ and prophesied while his people and his country were under siege from their enemies. Even so, Isaiah never wavered in his hope in God. In spite of betrayal, invasion, war, and exile, he trusted that God was the Master of the future and would eventually usher in a reign of justice and peace.

The second great figure of Advent, foretold in this reading, is John the Baptist. He, too, speaks to a demoralized people, this time living resentfully under Roman occupation. In contrast with the ancient Isaiah, John is the imminent preparation for the coming of God's Son. John fulfills the words of Isaiah's prophecy, and his message is the same as Isaiah's: Look to your lives now; tomorrow might be too late. Repent today and be converted. Change your hearts today and your whole world will change. See things in a new light: See them as God sees them — not as you find it convenient to see them. Look through the eyes of God.

And like Isaiah, John the Baptist speaks of the impossibility of divorcing faith from genuine social justice, from the duty to stand up for those who cannot speak for themselves. In our day, we would think immediately of children in the womb and the vulnerable elderly, the poor and the homeless, those who are starving and coping with the ravages of war, abuse, or addiction. John helps us in our preparation for the coming of Christ by calling us out of our complacency, our satisfaction with comfort and mediocrity, which keeps us from facing up to the challenge to change our lives. Whereas Isaiah looks from many centuries before to the eventual coming of a King, John speaks of the imminent arrival of One Who is greater than himself and Who will challenge settled perspectives and bring into men's hearts the fire of the Spirit.

The message is clear: We are to prepare for the celebration of the Birth of Jesus Christ at Christmas, and for the moment when Our Lord will return again in glory at the end of time, by repenting and turning away from all that separates us from God, from each other, and from our true selves—that is, by turning away from sin. The readings this week, and throughout Advent, bring us from the remote preparation of Isaiah, through the imminent preparation of John the Baptist, and to the immediate preparation of Mary, who gives birth to the Savior of the World.

PROPHETIC HONESTY

Fr. Ronald Creighton-Jobe, 2006

Little Oratory, London, England

It's very easy for us to want to be like everyone else out there. God chose His people to be uniquely His own, but very often they identified more readily with entirely worldly values. They wanted to be like the other nations — especially in the matter of kingship. The judges who helped Moses in his unenviable task of keeping the people of Israel faithful to the covenant discouraged the people from seeking kings. But God relented and gave them their king, and of course, the whole enterprise ended up being a mess from top to bottom.

We are often tempted, especially in today's world, to be like others. And yet we were summoned, chosen in

Baptism, to be in relationship, in a distinctive way, with a loving God. Having this great vocation, we should ask ourselves constantly as we examine our consciences, "Am I fulfilling my side of my covenant relationship with God?" Almost always, we have to admit that we are not.

That is why, in preparing for Christmas during this season of Advent, the importance of honesty with God is highlighted. It only makes sense, of course, to be honest to God because God knows everything about us. He knows our inmost thoughts and the secrets of our hearts. And yet so often we try to hide from Him. This is what happened in Israel. As the kings strayed further and further away from the ideal, there arose the prophets, who became more and more important in salvation history.

The prophets acted as the conscience of the people of Israel, exhorting them to return to faithfulness to the God Who loved them. What a difficult and dangerous vocation it was (and is) to be a prophet, having to speak truths that are extremely unpalatable to others — and to suffer for it. But this is part of the prophetic vocation — to accept the consequences of telling the truth. Another part of the prophetic vocation is to inspire the longing of God's people for the One Who would come to restore them to friendship with their Creator. Longing and love must go together.

I remember as a child longing to be baptized and begging my parents to let me. They probably thought I was very odd indeed, but I prayed for it for years. And then one day I encountered Venerable Fulton Sheen. He was preaching in the cathedral in Saint Louis, where I was a choirboy, and I was introduced to him. My future godmother told the bishop that I wanted to be baptized and said that he responded, "The first thing he must do is long for that above all things and pray for it." And that's what I did. And here I am today.

This is what the prophets do: They enable the people to long for God. There were many great prophets, and this process of longing and waiting and yearning went on for centuries. At the heart of this was the longing for the Savior, a King Who would restore Israel's relationship with God. Of course, they thought he would be as a political figure, a warrior, and many were surprised and even disappointed by the real thing.

But we should not be disappointed, because the prophets' message of repentance is central to our understanding of the hope and light that should inspire our Advent preparations.

We know that the Savior was a Babe, wrapped in swaddling clothes, vulnerable yet all powerful. Let us ask for the grace to long to be united with God, to realize more fully our baptismal calling, and to take up in our lives a sense of the prophetic nature of the Christian vocation.

Longing implies waiting, but in the modern world there is instant gratification of almost all our instincts, bad and good. A certain credit card once advertised that it "took the waiting out of wanting." What a dangerous motto! Part of the whole point of wanting is that we often have to exercise patience to receive what we long for. In this way, our love can grow for what is worthy, and fade for what is not. When we have instant gratification, this diminishes the value we place on the things we long for.

But in loving and trusting God, this can never be the case. He gives us at every moment of our lives exactly what we need. It is a beautiful paradox: He fulfills us, but at the same time He increases our longing for Him. God loves us so much that He wants us to long for Him.

The prophets came to communicate this truth, but prophecy ceased for many centuries in Israel. There were chastisements, exiles, returns, the rebuilding of the Temple, and many more dramas—but prophecy stopped, and the institutions of Israel were developed through the Scribes, the Pharisees, the teaching of the rabbis, and the law. This is an enormous difference between the old and the new dispensation: In the Old Covenant, the law, not longing and love, was the expression of fidelity.

But then the last of the great prophets arrived on the scene, and what an extraordinary figure he was. Each of the prophets had a particular outward sign to capture the imagination of their listeners. And this prophet, a man called John, had as his sign baptism, washing in the River Jordan, as a sign of repentance. It was John's great vocation to be the messenger chosen by God from his mother's womb to usher in the unthinkable.

John preached repentance. This is a very strong word; in Greek it is *metanoia*, a total change of the person. With God's grace, we have to turn ourselves inside out so that all our neediness, all our pain, all our vulnerability is there for God to heal. This baptism, of course, looked forward to our own Baptism. Our Baptism is an outward sign, too, but unlike John's, it actually brings about what it stands for, and we are objectively changed. It is symbolic, but *not only* symbolic. Our Baptism is what enables us, through grace, to continue the process of repentance from all that is not God.

The message of repentance is also a message of hope. It is comforting to acknowledge our neediness before God in trust and faith. We know that only He can heal that brokenness and fulfill that longing. John the Baptist is summoning us to radical transformation. Isn't it extraordinary: the last of the Old Testament preparing for the fulfillment?

Advent tells us that we must be honest with God, and to do that, we have to learn the virtue of humility. All the virtues are difficult, but with the grace of God, nothing is impossible. Humility, quite simply, is accepting this—accepting Who God is and who I am and what the difference is. Humility is the virtue that's necessary for all the others to flourish. And once we do that—and this is the lesson of Advent—we will be liberated.

The message of John the Baptist in the desert, in that place of freedom, is that, with repentance, with the washing away of sin, we will be able to stand before God in uprightness. That is true freedom, true hope, true humility. And John the Baptist died for that truth.

Let us pray that we will be a witness of the truth to others. And let us pray that the prophetic dimension of our baptismal vocation will be realized in our hearts.

Waiting for Christ with Christ

Fr. Pat Lombard, 2013

Cathedral of the Immaculate Conception, Sligo, Ireland

The Second Week of Advent very often includes the feast of the Immaculate Conception of the Blessed Virgin Mary, so let us begin with considering the sinless Mary. Defined as a dogma of the Church in 1854 by Pope Pius IX, this infallible teaching tells us that through a special grace and privilege from Almighty God and by virtue of the merits won by her Son, Mary was kept free from sin, including original sin, from the moment of her conception. She was given this unique privilege because God had marked her out to be the *Theotokos*, the God-bearer.

While the Immaculate Conception was officially defined in 1854, many Church Fathers affirmed this belief and in many places a feast celebrating it was observed from the seventh century onward. There is nothing new about the Immaculate Conception; the concept has been with us over the centuries.

As we think of Mary's sinlessness, we think of Mary as our mother, Mary who looks after us, Mary who is a model for us, Mary who places her arms around us to lead us. Every time we pray our Rosary and reflect on the life of Jesus, Mary leads us on a special journey of prayer to Him.

Remember in John's Gospel when Christ is on the Cross, and He looks down at the beloved disciple saying, "Behold, your mother" (John 19:27). We are also the beloved disciples of Jesus. He loves each and every one of us in a special way, so He says to each of us as well, "Behold, your mother." And so as we reflect on this wonderful feast of Mary, we know that by celebrating her and her care for us we can invite her to sanctify our homes, to support our families, and to help our communities by leading us to Jesus and helping us to love Him more and more.

Now let us turn to this Second Sunday of Advent, beginning with this week's selection from Isaiah,[11] in which he speaks of a future King:

[11] Lectionary Cycle A.

> There shall come forth a shoot from the stump of
> Jesse, and a branch shall grow out of his roots. And
> the Spirit of the LORD shall rest upon him, the spirit
> of wisdom and understanding, the spirit of counsel
> and might, the spirit of knowledge and the fear of
> the LORD. (Isa. 11:1–2)

Isaiah is addressing his people in their own context, but so
much of that history is applicable to us today. Isaiah saw
so many people forgetting about God. He saw strife, the
extreme pursuit of wealth, the struggles his people were
enduring, the armies targeting other countries, the political intrigue — and through it all he saw people relying on
themselves and other people instead of on God.

Isaiah could see that if we take God out of the equation,
mankind will end up doing away with mankind. What could
happen to the people of Israel but destruction? But Isaiah
also knew the God that loved and cared for His people. He
knew that God wanted to intervene and to help. And when
His people would come back to Him and be more open to
His presence, He would intervene in an extraordinary way.

In this little piece of Scripture, Isaiah predicts the future
King — a new King, a new Messiah that people could look
forward to. The Spirit of God would rest upon them and a

new era would come—one of peace and joy for those who are persecuted. But for those who persecute and oppress, it would be a time of judgment.

But the people grew weary of waiting. They had experienced so many hardships: the exile in Babylon, the destruction of Jerusalem, the razing of the Temple. And so the people were fearful and many forgot that God had promised He would come—until John the Baptist appeared on the scene. This Sunday we hear about John fulfilling Isaiah's prophecy that a forerunner would precede the Messiah as he says, "Repent, for the kingdom of heaven is at hand" (Matt. 3:2).

When John came, he wore a shirt of camel hair—nothing fancy, just the ordinary clothes of the desert. People came, though, because his message was so real, so authentic. And so people listened to him. Even the Pharisees and the Scribes, we are told, came to hear him, and the people listened and they believed and they waited.

And the Messiah came, but, as we know, He was rejected by the very men who were waiting for Him. Now, we wait for the Messiah to come again. At His Ascension, Jesus told His disciples that He would be back. We don't know when, but we know that one day He will come in glory. Will we be ready?

Christ, in the meantime, hasn't left us orphans. Through the power of the Holy Spirit, Jesus is with us always through the sacraments of the Church and most especially through the Eucharist, the sacrament of God's abiding love for us always.

When Jesus hung on the Cross and uttered, "I thirst," He was thirsting for our love (John 19:28). He was saying, "See how much I love you. Will you respond by loving me back?" The vinegar the soldiers offered to Him was horrible stuff. Jesus was not, and is not, looking for that. He is not looking for the vinegar of our indifference. No, He is looking for us to love Him sincerely, now and always, and to love our neighbor, especially the poor and the needy, as we love ourselves. How difficult is that? Yet if we journey in the love of Jesus, we will experience not only His care but also His grace to embrace our brothers and sisters throughout the world, who can experience, through us, the care of Jesus. They in turn may well be our welcoming party at the gates of Heaven.

Now is the season of preparation, of learning to grow in that love as we meditate on His first coming and prepare for His second coming. We can know and experience His presence with us in the life of the Church, in our prayer, and in our love for one another. Sometimes, though, in the darkness of our lives He may seem absent. Yet he is always close to us, looking for an opening into our hearts to encourage, enlighten, correct, and forgive.

These are the opportunities of grace that He offers to us. He wishes us to know how precious we are to Him and how much He wants to help us. This is the beautiful opportunity Advent offers to us: learning to entrust our lives to Him, as, through our Church, He gives Himself to us now in preparation for His glorious return. And when He does come—and we do not know when—He will embrace us in the most special way possible, bringing His eternal love and life to all who wait for Him.

THIRD WEEK OF ADVENT

Trust and Renewal in Christ

Archbishop Michael Neary, 2004

Ballintubber Abbey, County Mayo, Ireland

At this point in the Advent season, the liturgy raises our minds and hearts beyond the routine, focusing us on God and the initiative He takes in our lives. The readings for this Third Sunday[12] are full of the conviction that the coming Messiah will bring about a change that is deep and widespread. God will re-create and renew all things. And yet, in our moments of world-weariness, we often feel too exhausted and even cynical to allow this power of God to possess us. Newness is possible, but it depends on God and is brought about by Jesus Christ.

[12] Lectionary Cycle A.

The Second Reading this Sunday comes from the Epistle of St. James (5:7–10), where we see this great saint encouraging us in a very practical way to allow Christ's newness to permeate all of life. St. James says, "You also be patient. Establish your hearts, for the coming of the Lord is at hand" (5:8). We can sense here a buoyant hope in spite of all the obstacles and daily sufferings we endure. As people of hope, Christians are distinguished, on the one hand, from the despairing, who believe that nothing can or will change, and, on the other hand, from the self-righteous and self-sufficient, who believe that they will be the vehicles of change themselves.

This week's reading from Isaiah (35:1–6a, 10) underlines the fact that without God's powerful Word and Presence, both creation and dysfunctional humanity are doomed. At the very center, this reading is the emphasis on God's Word, and on His coming in power to save us. In our era of mistrust and insecurity and vulnerability, full of fragile peace and broken promises, Isaiah's description of "weak hands," "feeble knees," and "fearful hearts" hits home (35:3–4). So many of us have that sense of being overwhelmed by fear, by timidity, by vulnerability, and simply by the lack of capacity to live a fully human life.

When the good news of God's coming is announced, the impact on the disabled and the dysfunctional is immediate and dramatic: "Then the eyes of the blind shall be opened, and the ears of the deaf unstopped; then shall the lame man leap like a hart, and the tongue of the dumb sing for joy" (Isa. 35:5–6). People are given back their lives. Humanity is restored to its fullness. God does what the world thinks is impossible. He is the One Who liberates us from the power of sin and heals the hurt that we cause to ourselves and to each other.

So much in our culture today encourages a focus on the self, on "self-fulfillment." But when the self becomes the center of all attention, people easily become disillusioned and despondent. All our insecurities and insufficiencies are laid bare. One beautiful effect of praying the psalms is that they focus us on God. This can be very therapeutic: By focusing on God, the pressure we place on ourselves is revealed.

The Responsorial Psalm today (146:6c–7, 8–9a, 9b–10) addresses our vulnerability and our insecurity by focusing on God, who keeps faith forever, Who is just to the oppressed, Who gives lavishly, Who liberates, Who heals, Who supports, Who protects, Who defends, and Who forgives. This is the God we worship, and this is the God Whom we await in this Advent, the God Who takes a special interest in and acts on behalf of the downtrodden, the vulnerable, the powerless, and the despairing.

In this week's Gospel (Matt. 11:2–11), we read of John the Baptist's request for confirmation of Jesus' identity, and who among us doesn't identify with that doubt? We are living two thousand years after the Birth of Christ, and we know quite a bit about unfulfilled expectations and shattered dreams. John the Baptist was a prophet, sent by God, to prepare the way for His Son—and yet he found himself in Herod's prison.

Jesus had not presented the Kingdom of God in the stark terms that John had anticipated—that is, as a time when the oppressors of God's people (the Roman occupiers, especially) would be punished—and this caused many to reject His claim to be the Messiah. You can sense some of this disillusionment in John. Here he was, the prophet of the Lord, locked up in prison, while the One who sets prisoners free was walking the streets nearby. John is understandably puzzled and confused. So he sent some of his disciples to Jesus to ask Him, point blank, if He is the One they had all be waiting for.

Jesus replied, directly referencing the words of the prophet Isaiah that we hear in the first reading. Jesus' miracles pointed to the way God was preparing His people — by reaching out to the lonely, the ostracized, and the downtrodden. In this way, Jesus presented Himself as the One Who fulfills the Old

Testament prophecies—a favorite theme of this particular Gospel writer.

After Jesus had interpreted His own ministry for John, He went on to interpret the ministry of John for the crowds. He reminds them that they had gone out to John in the wilderness for a specific purpose: They were looking for prophetic signs of redemption and salvation. They were not merely concerned about "a reed shaken by the wind," a symbol of weakness and indecision (Matt. 11:7). They were looking for solidity and permanence, and they had found in John the Baptist not just a prophet, but a bridge connecting the old and the new. John was an Old Testament figure standing on the threshold of the New.

John's questions, of course, really are our questions. And we, too, in a less dramatic way, span the gap between the past and the future; part of our baptismal calling is to pass down the Faith across the divides of time and culture. John may be speaking for those who were once sure of their faith but are now not so sure. He may be speaking for those who are impressed by the accomplishments of Jesus but, at the same time, wonder whether the ultimate meaning of things can be brought to a satisfactory fulfillment by gentleness and meekness in a world where there's so much cruelty and where so few have so much power.

The pressure of events and the ways of the world force such questions on honest minds: "Is there really a God Who cares? Does this God have a plan for the world, a plan for you and for me? If so, is Jesus Christ the revelation of that God, or should we look elsewhere for answers to ultimate questions?"

The answer Jesus gives is the testament of His own life, and His fulfillment of the words of the prophets. If that was good enough for John the Baptist, it can be good enough for us.

Rejoice in God's Presence

Fr. Vincent Twomey, 2008

St. Peter's Church, National Shrine of
St. Oliver Plunkett, Drogheda, Ireland

Joy is the theme of the Third Sunday of Advent, Gaudete Sunday, which gets its name from the Introit of the Mass: "Rejoice always in the Lord" (Phil. 4:4). In the Second Reading today, Paul repeats the call: "Rejoice always!" (1 Thess. 5:16). How realistic is his call?

To this, my first answer is: Lourdes. Why? There, one experiences something of the joy of which St. Paul spoke over and over again. Lourdes reverses the order of our secular world, where wealth, money, health, and status seem to be the only values that count. In Lourdes, the sick, the poor, the little ones of this world — like the young seer

Bernadette herself—are the prized ones. And they radiate joy. That is the ever-present miracle of Lourdes—indeed, of our faith.

Central to any pilgrimage is Confession. One of the great graces many find in Lourdes is the gift of repentant tears. There is no joy like that of a repentant sinner, who tastes God's infinite love and mercy, who experiences that peace that the world cannot take away, the peace of Christ.

Our Lord says that those who mourn will be consoled (Matt. 5:4). Blessed are those who mourn their own sins, because God is drawn to the contrite and brokenhearted (see Ps. 51:17). But also blessed are those who mourn the sins of others—that is, those who are saddened by the spiritual damage sin does to others and whose sadness is a prayer for their repentance.

There is, however, another kind of mourning that is not blessed: Scripture refers to it as the "sorrow of the world" (see 2 Cor. 7:10). According to St. Paul, this kind of mourning leads to death, specifically in the form of boredom and its related vice—sloth, or spiritual inertia. These are often the products of secularism, with its theoretical and practical denial of God. Boredom may be one of the defining characteristics of our age, the product of the dominant assumption that nothing is sacred, that nothing really matters.

Boredom is the experience of indifference. Life no longer tastes good; or, rather, everything tastes the same. Despair is never far from the surface in today's society, frequently manifesting itself in the form of consumerist excess and workaholism and addiction. These all arise from a sense of helplessness and a desire to escape. And the modern entertainment industry feeds off this boredom, trying to assuage it with constant stimuli that are subject to the law of diminishing returns. As a result, entertainment must become ever louder and more frenetic to distract people, as Pope Benedict XVI would say, from the spiritual void in the depths of their hearts.

The antidote to boredom is the humble acceptance of our true greatness and dignity, of our vocation to full communion with God, of the fact that we are loved by God with a passionate love. Once we submit to God's love, revealed in the Face of Christ, we know true and lasting joy. The assurance of that joy is what we celebrate on Gaudete Sunday, the joy that alone can answer the deepest longings of the human soul.

The earliest evidence we have of human life demonstrates a deep concern with the sacred, especially those ritual sites associated with our passage from this world to the next. G. K. Chesterton never failed to express his own amazement at the evidence of such profound reverence for the sacred found in earliest traces of human life on earth. Our ancestors fervently desired to know the transcendent Other, to see His face. Their idols were expressions, however disordered, of the desire written into the DNA of all people to see the Face of God.

The Old Testament gave voice to the human desire to see the Face of God: "It is your face that I seek, O Lord, hide not your face" (Ps. 27:8). And yet, when eventually God did show His Face, His chosen people didn't recognize Him. He was a great disappointment. Even John the Baptist was tempted to doubt, as we heard in today's Gospel.

As John languished in Herod's filthy jail with the threat of death hanging over his head, he sent his disciples to Jesus to ask what the great German exegete Heinrich Schlier called the Advent question: "Are you he who is to come, or shall we look for another?" (Matt. 11:3). This is the question that arises in the hearts of all believers at some stage in our lives, above all when affliction seems to overwhelm us, when human hopes fade, and when our daily joys evaporate—when God seems to have hidden His Face.

The important thing is that John turned to the Lord in his existential predicament—perhaps we could say in his dark night of the soul. He didn't despair or rebel. John's expectations might have been shattered, but he still looked to Jesus to help him out of his anguish. Jesus gave John's disciples a paradoxical answer:

> Go and tell John what you hear and see: the blind receive their sight and the lame walk, lepers are cleansed and the deaf hear, and the dead are raised up, and the poor have good news preached to them. And blessed is he who takes no offense at me. (Matt. 11:4–6, with reference to Isa. 35:5–6; 61:1)

In other words, blessed is he who will not be shocked by the One Who came, as Isaiah himself foretold, as the Suffering Servant (see Isa. 52:13–15; Zech. 12:10).

In Hebrew, *Shekinah* means the presence of God among His people, such as His appearing in a cloud over the Tabernacle (see Exod. 40:34). Rabbinical tradition, which coined the term, came eventually to understand the *Shekinah* as the act of God's sharing in the lot of His people, first when they went into slavery in Egypt, and later when they went into exile in Babylon. The burning bush (Exod. 3:2) was interpreted as the revelation of God's Presence in the lowliest plant in the forest, the thorn bush, and it was seen as a symbol of God's Presence with His chosen people when they felt most abandoned by Him: He was present to them in their suffering, as He was in the burning thorn bush.

Though the prophets would not have been surprised, no one expected God would one day end up being crowned with thorns.

Advent is the time when we enter more deeply into the mystery of God's presence with us — that is, when the Word became flesh and dwelt among us so that we could share in His divinity (see 2 Pet. 1:4). This is the source of our joy, which transcends all ephemeral earthly joys.

This joy is the true mark of the Christian martyrs, as can be seen in St. Oliver Plunkett. Though innocent, he was found guilty of treason and condemned to the most gruesome of deaths by being hanged, drawn, and quartered at Tyburn, London. There must have been times when he, too, felt abandoned by God. But the night before he was to be executed, we are told, he slept like a newborn babe, and the following day he went to his horrendous death with a smile on his lips.

God never deserts us, even when we feel abandoned by Him: That is the joy we celebrate on the Third Sunday of Advent.

In Joyful Hope

Fr. Stewart Foster, 2010

St. Anthony of Padua Church, Rye, England

"Rejoice in the Lord always; again I will say, Rejoice."
These are the words of St. Paul in his Letter to the Philippians (4:4), which are borrowed for the traditional entrance
antiphon for this Sunday. There is an unmistakable note
of joy and expectation in the Scripture readings and other
texts used in the Mass this week,[13] a joy marked also by the
rose-colored vestments that the priest may wear.

What is the reason for this joyful hope? I invite you to
think of that point during the Mass, after we have recited
the Lord's Prayer in preparation for Holy Communion,

[13] Lectionary Cycle A.

when the priest's prayer concludes, "as we wait in joyful hope for the coming of Our Savior, Jesus Christ."

Our lives here on earth must be a constant, joy-filled preparation for that final meeting with Christ, when our hope will be fulfilled. Our joy, therefore, is one of anticipation and expectation, a readiness to greet the coming of Christ, Who makes all things new. It is Jesus Christ Who is the true and only source of our waiting in joyful hope; and it is Christ Who is the goal, the final destination of our hope.

We can see this in the reading from Isaiah and its fulfillment in Matthew this Sunday. The prophet lays out the signs of the age of the Messiah: "Then the eyes of the blind shall be opened, and the ears of the deaf unstopped; then shall the lame man leap like a hart, and the tongue of the dumb sing for joy" (Isa. 35:5–6). Like all the prophets of the Old Testament, Isaiah speaks to us in our time, because what God foretold through him has now been realized. The longed-for Messiah has come among us: This and every prophecy is fulfilled in Jesus of Nazareth, God made man, our Savior.

And we see this very precisely in the selection from the Gospel of Matthew (11:2–11). St. John the Baptist, then languishing in prison, sent his own disciples to ask Jesus if He was the long-expected Messiah. This was a crucial question for the followers of the Baptist, and it must not remain consigned to a merely historical or academic interest in our times. The question of whether Jesus really is Who He says is every bit as relevant, especially in a world that is so often indifferent, if not hostile, to genuine faith.

For Christians, it's important to ask ourselves what sort of Messiah we expect. How is the Chosen One, the Anointed of God, to be recognized? Our Lord tells John's messengers to open their eyes and to look around them — to witness the blind seeing and the deaf hearing, as Isaiah foretold — and then to report their observations. The Messiah is not a figure of anger or power, of human sophistication or pride. On the contrary, He is the One Who blesses the needy, Who heals the sick, Who raises the dead. The Gospel is proclaimed to the poor, and, says Jesus, "Blessed is he who takes no offense at me" (Matt. 11:6).

As followers of Jesus, we are called to remain faithful not to the things of the world, in the sense of placing our trust in that which is passing, or transitory, but to Our Lord Himself, to Jesus Christ. This is a message, indeed a challenge, that each of us needs to discover and to meet daily, a truth echoed clearly in the Scripture readings today, a truth that must be affirmed again and again, not least during Advent.

Having spoken to the disciples of John the Baptist about the Messiah, Jesus goes on to speak about John himself. John is something of a stark, even a harsh, figure, but he is equally a man of joyful hope. St. John Henry Newman, in reflecting upon St. John the Baptist, wrote these words:

> The Holy Baptist was separated from the world. He ... called it to repentance. Then went out all Jerusalem to him in the desert and he confronted it face-to-face. But in his teaching he spoke of "One" who should come to them ... in a far different way. He should not separate Himself from them, he should not display Himself as some higher being but as their brother, as their own flesh and bone, as One among many brethren, as One of the multitude and amidst them; nay, He was among them already.... "There hath stood in your midst, One you knew not." That Greater One called Himself the Son of Man—He was content to be taken as ordinary in all respects, though He was the Highest. The Baptist says, "There is in the midst of you One Whom you know not."[14]

---

[14] *Meditations on Christian Doctrine*.

John the Baptist is the model of humility because he points not to himself but to Jesus Christ, Who enters our midst even if He is so often unrecognized. What's more, John makes it plain that everything good, including the truth he relates to the people of Jerusalem, comes from God. We are instruments of His grace. That is why John the Baptist is a man of joyful hope, despite the fact that he was imprisoned and later martyred: he knew what and Whom his life was for. It is the very starkness of John the Baptist and his message of repentance that allows us to see the light of Christ shining more clearly in and through the prophet's words and actions.

St. Augustine made exactly the same point about John, reminding us that the Baptist's words came from the Word, that he was the lamp and not the Light. This is our vocation, too: humbly to reflect the Truth and Light of Christ, not to develop the pride that thinks we are the source of goodness. This pride smothers Christ's Light; it is the opposite of the Truth.

The rejoicing of Advent is focused precisely on the real truth: that we await in hope the coming of the One Who, born in poverty and humility and facing many dangers, takes upon Himself the frailty of our human nature. He is the One Who alone has the power to restore us to communion and to friendship with God, for the Babe of Bethlehem is the One Who will suffer and die for our sake, Who by means of His Passion, His Death, and His Resurrection has redeemed the world. The Crib and the Cross can never be separated.

The Incarnation is redemptive. And then, at the close of the age it is the very same Jesus Christ, now seated in glory at the right hand of the Father, Who will return to Judge both the living and the dead. Advent encapsulates all of this: the beginning and the end, memory and expectation, hope and joy.

As St. James reminds us in the Second Reading at Mass (5:7–10), we must be patient, preparing for the coming of the Lord by remaining faithful to Him, just like the farmer who waits for the fruits of the earth to spring up, confident that the rain and the sun will nurture and bring to completion the seed he has sown. "Do not grumble, brethren . . . ; behold, the Judge is standing at the doors" (James 5:9).

In the season of Advent, the Church offers each one of us a privileged time to prepare for the coming of Christ. We can use this time best by listening to the Word of God in Holy Scripture, by spending time each day in personal prayer, by attending Mass on Sunday and any other times during the week that we may be able to do so, by seeking to be of greater service to our neighbor, and especially by ensuring that we make a good and sincere Confession in time for Christmas. In each of these ways, and by remaining always united in prayer with our Blessed Lady, the Mother of our Redeemer, we are being called to live in joyful hope, ready to welcome Jesus Christ with joy at Christmas.

HEALING OUR SENSES
AND OUR SOULS

Fr. Shane Gallagher, 2013

Cathedral of the Immaculate Conception, Sligo, Ireland

"The blind receive their sight and the lame walk ... and the deaf hear" (Matt. 11:5). These are three of the signs of the Messiah foretold by the prophet Isaiah in this Sunday's First Reading (Isa. 35:1–6a, 10) that are mentioned by Jesus in this week's Gospel (Matt. 11:2–11). Let us begin our reflection on this week in Advent by exploring these three miracles.

On several occasions, such as the beautiful meeting with Bartimaeus (Mark 10:46–52), Jesus granted sight to those who were physically blind. But Jesus also encountered and cured spiritual blindness, which is a blindness of mind and a dullness of sense. When a person ignores common sense and resists a well-reasoned argument pointing him clearly to the truth, then it would be fair to say that that person has some degree of spiritual blindness.

The modern world takes full advantage of spiritual blindness by sophistry, which is the use of clever but false arguments with the intention of deceiving. It was a tactic used by false philosophers in ancient Greece to trick impressionable minds into immoral living. One example of this was during the recent Irish abortion referendum, when theatrics and the manipulative use of words created a false compassion for those who desired abortion to be legal, and took the focus away from the defenseless unborn. If a person is not praying and consulting the Holy Spirit, he will become spiritually blind and thus susceptible to this kind of sophistry.

The remedy for spiritual blindness lies in Jesus and in the sacraments of the Church. I once knew of an old priest who was particularly blessed with the gift of discernment. He would spend long periods in front of Jesus in Eucharistic Adoration; the Holy Mass was the center of his priestly existence; and he went to Confession regularly. Young and old would come to him, day and night, looking for advice and spiritual counsel.

This old priest, it turned out, was physically blind. And yet people could sense that he could very often see the world and their situations much more clearly than they could. Eucharistic Adoration had compensated him richly with spiritual sight; indeed, he knew exactly the kind of sight that Jesus was referring to in St. Matthew's Gospel. Let us ask God during this Advent to grant us that spiritual sight so that we will be able to navigate the twists and turns and sophistry of a confused and deceitful world. A vibrant Catholic sacramental life keeps the scales away from our eyes, enabling us to make good choices.

Let's turn now to restoring hearing to the deaf, removing another obstacle to the senses. We live in a very noisy world, and sometimes we become so engrossed in that noise that we become deaf to the Word of God. I recall witnessing a skit some children put on at a youth retreat a number of years ago. A young man, positioned at one side of the stage, played the role of Jesus and called out to a young woman at the center. She was surrounded by several other young people who were dressed all in black who were roaring in her ear, representing the noisy distractions of the world—and, of course, drowning out Christ and stopping her from encountering Him. This, with smartphones and television and social media, is what happens so often today.

It was an effective way of illustrating the deafness that Jesus wishes to eradicate in this noisy contemporary existence.

It is said that empty vessels make the most noise. Well, let's turn to the largest empty vessel of all: Satan. He wants every human soul to be so engrossed in the empty clamor of the world that we forget that God exists and that He loves us. In so doing, we forget the Gospel and the fact that He has a wondrous plan for each and every one of us. Satan has nothing to offer any soul but emptiness, yet he creates so much noise that we fail to recognize not only God but also the evil one. C. S. Lewis pointed out that Satan's greatest trick is to convince people that he doesn't exist.

There is a story about a young man called Karol Wojtyla, who, during the Second World War, was part of a youth drama society in Poland and would recite old Polish stories and poetry to keep the culture alive. One day, when young Karol was reciting a Polish poem for his friends, a Nazi truck with a loudspeaker came past the house, blaring Nazi propaganda. But the young Wojtyla did not even flinch: He continued calmly to recite the poem to the finish and would not allow the propaganda to interrupt his world. This young boy was grounded in prayer, and he became the great Pope St. John Paul II. This holy man would not allow noise to direct the course of his life.

Perhaps this is one reason for the drop in vocations to the priesthood and to the religious life in the Western world: Young people no longer hear God speak to them. Advent is a time to heed the words from the psalmist: "Be still and know that I am God" (Ps. 46:10).

When we pray with Scripture, we begin to see that each word and phrase has a deeper significance than we first thought. Blindness, deafness, and lameness are everyday realities, yet Our Lord used them to explain powerfully what it is that He was sent to do.

Let's turn, finally, to the healing of the lame. To be lame—that is, to be unable to walk—is to be stuck. Walking represents progress, both in the world around us and in our souls. Often, though, we are grounded by our circumstances or choices, and we feel as if we are going nowhere.

There is a lovely line from St. John's Gospel, though, that should give us hope. Jesus declares, "I came that they may have life, and have it abundantly" (John 10:10). Jesus wants us to walk with Him spiritually, and in doing so, we will not merely survive but thrive. As a priest, I meet so many people who have stopped walking with Jesus. They are lame, grounded by addictions, depression, despair, dysfunctional relationships, idolatry, and so many other crippling weights. They are merely surviving, not thriving.

Every year, millions of pilgrims make for the dusty roads of Spain, Portugal, and France as they attempt the Camino de Santiago. Walking the Camino, like any pilgrimage, represents spiritual progress. A feeling of achievement energizes pilgrims as they move through the towns and villages, nearing the destination of Santiago de Compostela, where St. James is said to be buried. The Camino is a mirror of life: We pray and talk to one another as we walk, rest, eat, laugh, and cry.

There is nothing more beautiful than seeing a young person going to Confession on a roadside in Spain along the route. Acknowledging our sinful, broken past and renewing our commitment to God: This is the way we get out of the rut and start moving again. And the pilgrimage we are all on is the greatest one of all: the pilgrimage to Heaven. To be lame is to be grounded in mediocrity, to live as if true progress toward God is not possible. Our Lord Jesus desires that we follow the signposts set out for us—the star that leads us to Him and His heavenly home. Advent is a time for walking again so that we can meet him—again—on Christmas Day and accompany Him thereafter.

Advent—and our pilgrimage of faith—is a journey. While we trek toward Christmas Day, we must remember that the journey does not stop there. We will be tested and tried like gold in a furnace, and we will need resolve. But we should take heart that the Lord will journey with us as often as we call on Him from our hearts.

FOURTH WEEK OF ADVENT

THE LIBERATION OF LOVE

Archbishop Michael Neary, 2004

Ballintubber Abbey, County Mayo, Ireland

In this Fourth Week of Advent, we are very close to Christmas and to the Birth of the Baby. The Church tries to show us in this time that, on the one hand, Jesus is in continuity with God's plan in the Old Testament and brings those plans to completion while, on the other hand, Jesus breaks out of all attempts to categorize Him. St. Paul writes to the Ephesians, trying to describe Christ Jesus: "For [God] has made known to us in all wisdom and insight the mystery of his will, according to his purpose which he set forth in Christ as a plan for the fulness of time, to unite all things in him, things in heaven and things on earth" (Eph. 1:9–10). So, while Jesus is the son of David in continuity with the old promises, He is also the Son of God in power through His Resurrection.

In the first reading this week, from the prophet Isaiah, we witness the tension not only between the prophet and the king but also within our own experience. There is a confrontation between two contrasting worlds, between two opposing systems of psychological security — that of this world and that of the spiritual realm. The prophet has given an assurance that faith will save, even in a seemingly worldly political crisis. The king, however, like us so often, is reluctant to submit his will to the claims of faith. This is a great temptation in each one of us: to act with foolish autonomy.

In this reading, the prophet announces a sign: A young woman will give birth to a child whose name is Immanuel, "God with us." Everything changes when God is with us. You can feel this in a small way if you have an opportunity to savor beautiful scenery or an environment that makes a special impact on you.

The Birth of the Baby is a sign of salvation and deliverance, which will come not through political alliance, but rather through reliance on the intervention of God, Who keeps His promises. Isaiah was addressing a situation in which people were tempted to form alliances with foreign powers, but he emphasized that it is reliance on God that will be the saving grace. And the same is true for us today: It is grace, not worldly practicality, that saves us.

As we edge closer to the celebration of the coming of Jesus, the reading from St. Paul's Letter to the Romans (1:1–7) focuses on the Davidic descent of Jesus. Paul identifies himself as a "servant of Jesus Christ, called to be an apostle." This is not something that he has chosen himself; rather, he was chosen by God. He affirms that the Gospel was "promised beforehand through his prophets in the holy scriptures," underlining the fact that God has kept and will keep His promises. This connects with the theme of the First Sunday of Advent: the continuity between Christ and those who had gone before Him, and the way He brings to fulfillment the promises of old.

The Apostle makes two assertions about Jesus Christ: that He "was descended from David according to the flesh and designated Son of God in power according to the Spirit of holiness by his resurrection from the dead." We must maintain the balance between those two aspects of Christ: the human and the divine, the fleshly and the spiritual, the Son of Mary and the Son of God. To emphasize one at the expense of the other means that we are not true to the reality of the Messiah. It is through Jesus Christ and

His coworkers, among them Paul, that the "obedience of faith" is brought to all believers. This truth in faith is meant for all, not just the apostles and other leaders: We all receive our faith as a calling from God.

In the Gospel reading today from St. Matthew (1:18–24), you'll notice that the evangelist is concerned with the conception and the naming of Jesus. These details serve to identify who Jesus is and what He does. The conception is described from the perspective of Joseph, this righteous man who repeatedly obeys the counsel of God's messenger. It becomes clear to Joseph that this conception is the work of God; Jesus is the product of a new and startling divine initiative. He acts distinctively as the Agent of the Divine Spirit, and He manifestly illustrates the unique power of God. The virginal conception signals the beginning of the fulfillment of God's saving purposes and ushers in a totally new age. It is long expected and hoped for, and yet it comes in a fashion so unusual that it could not possibly have been anticipated.

Christ's naming also calls attention to His place in history. The angel directs Joseph to call the child by the name "Jesus," followed by an explanation, "For He will save His people from their sins." This alerts us to the peculiar role this Infant will play, which will unfold in His ministry and particularly in His Death and Resurrection. He is the Messiah, Who heals divisions, Who reconciles all of us to God and to one another: This Baby will do what only God can do. And so, wherever the name of Jesus appears, there is the absolute assurance of God's forgiveness.

The text of today's Gospel gives Jesus another name: Emmanuel, "God with us." Wherever Jesus is, God is there, present with His people. This idea comes through at the beginning and the end of Matthew's Gospel (the Great Commission), but also midway through, when Jesus reminds His disciples: "For where two or three are gathered in my name, there am I in the midst of them" (Matt. 18:20). Jesus is not a figure confined to the past. He is the presence of God; He is accompanying His Church in Her mission; He energizes His Church in Her teaching; He pioneers Her efforts to make disciples of all nations.

How does this Gospel relate to you and me? Joseph received a specific message in the Gospel that began with the greeting "Do not fear." Indeed, this is the most frequently repeated command in the whole Bible: "Do not be afraid." As we draw ever closer to Christmas, that exhortation could be a significant aspect of our prayer and preparation.

Now, this does not mean that parents should not be concerned about where their teenage children are hanging out, nor does it mean that children should not be afraid if their parents are cruel or otherwise dysfunctional. At times we have very good reasons to fear immediate danger or distress.

But St. John reminds us that perfect love casts out fear (1 John 4:18). And so the question is, "How do we reach perfect love?" This is where the Christmas message enters. The essence of the Christmas story is that God is with us *in a particular and unique way.* He is with us to save us; this is what the name "Jesus" means.

And so there is liberation—from sin, of course, but also from the destructive implications and results of sin, freedom from the fear that keeps us from loving God with our whole hearts, minds, and souls and from loving one another. The antidote to our fears is the knowledge and the confidence that "God is with us." Our response to this Christmas gift must surely be one of trust, letting the Lord gradually remove the fears that get in the way of perfect love.

I believe that all too many Christians may be afraid of God—not the holy fear that is a gift of the Spirit, but a cowering fear that paralyzes them. In their experience, God seems to be so distant, so majestic, so uncaring. If this is our image of God, then we need to look into the Crib or at the Cross. This is our God: in swaddling clothes or nailed to a tree.

Further, all too many Christians are afraid of themselves: reluctant to trust their own joy, afraid to be happy. They think that if they are too happy, something bad will happen to them. But remember the promise of Jesus: "I will see you again and your hearts will rejoice, and no one will take your joy from you" (John 16:22).

Many Christians are also afraid to risk, like the fearful servant in the Gospel parable who was afraid to invest his master's capital (Matt. 25:14–30). He kept the money in a safe place and ventured nothing, only to hear his master say, "You wicked and lazy servant." We are called, rather, to go forth in confidence, spreading the light and grace of Christ even when it feels as if it might be costly.

Christmas is not an end to all fear, but it should be the beginning of a fresh love for a God, Who experienced in His flesh all that we experience; a fresh love for ourselves, for what God has achieved in and through us; a fresh love for our sisters and brothers, for each image of God that we touch each day, with a word or a telephone call or a decision or a prayer.

In this last week before the divine Baby is born, let us meditate on this love and try to identify where it can cast out our fear.

FULL OF GRACE

Bishop Alan Hopes, 2005

St. Etheldreda Church, Ely Place, London, England

We are so close to Christmas now, and so we need to be particularly alert to the One Who is coming. The liturgy for the Fourth Sunday of Advent[15] is like the vigil for a feast because we know that the time of waiting is nearly over. In the Gospel this week, we hear Luke's account of the fulfillment of the promise of Isaiah: "And behold, you will conceive in your womb and bear a son, and you shall call his name Jesus" (Luke 1:31). This week, we fix our eyes on the manger.

[15] Lectionary Cycle B.

But we must not lose sight of the fact that this Birth is just the first stage in the new history of salvation, which will be consummated only in the Heavenly Kingdom. Recognizing and integrating this immanence and transcendence, this particularity and wholeness, is characteristic of the liturgy: It always celebrates the entirety of the mystery of faith, which is indivisible, even when it seems to be dealing with only one facet. The liturgy draws us toward the final stage, the great consummation of the end of time.

In the First Reading today (2 Sam. 7:1–5, 8b–12, 14a, 16), we hear of King David, who wants to build the Lord a temple where He may dwell. And in the Gospel (Luke 1:26–38), we see how God Himself prepares His temple in the form of Mary, who will be the place where He first comes to dwell among His people. Therefore, this week we are focusing on Mary as the one in whom the hope of the ages is fulfilled and in whom a new hope dawns.

Mary is the third figure of Advent preparing us for the coming of the Lord. We have journeyed from the eventual coming of the King in Isaiah, through the imminent coming of the King in John the Baptist, to the immediate coming of the King in Mary. In her single-minded dedication and her readiness to give God priority over everything else in her life, she becomes the channel through whom our world and our lives have been transformed.

As Mary read the Jewish Scriptures, she must have pondered the words of the prophet Isaiah and the immeasurable greatness of God. She knew enough about God to know that He would do what He said. And so, when God called, her reply was simple and direct: "Behold, I am the handmaid of the Lord; let it be to me according to your word." (Luke 1:38). St. Bernard has written a beautiful reflection on the Annunciation of the Savior to Mary:

> The whole world awaits her answer to God, for the world is waiting for its redeemer.... You have heard, O Virgin, that you will conceive and bear a son; you have heard that it will not be by man but by the Holy Spirit. The angel awaits an answer; it is time for him to return to God who sent him. We too are waiting, O Lady, for your word of compassion; the sentence of condemnation weighs heavily upon us. The price of our salvation is offered to you. We shall be set free at once if you consent. In the eternal Word of God we all came to be, and behold, we die. In your brief response we are to be remade in order to be recalled to life. Tearful Adam

with his sorrowing family begs this of you, O loving Virgin, in their exile from Paradise. Abraham begs it, David begs it. All the other holy patriarchs, your ancestors, ask it of you, as they dwell in the country of the shadow of death. This is what the whole earth waits for, prostrate at your feet. It is right in doing so, for on your word depends comfort for the wretched, ransom for the captive, freedom for the condemned, indeed, salvation for all the sons of Adam, the whole of your race. Answer quickly, O Virgin. Reply in haste to the angel, or rather through the angel to the Lord. Answer with a word, receive the Word of God. Speak your own word, conceive the divine Word. Breathe a passing word, embrace the eternal Word.

And Mary responds, as we all know so well in our very souls, with her *fiat*.

In the two great themes of this Gospel reading—the gift of the Spirit and Mary's response—we see how the grace of God, given at such costs, can transform a human life until it becomes full of glory. This is the fulfillment of our Advent hope. By the grace of the Spirit two thousand years ago, Mary was enabled to make her perfect response and be faithful to God throughout her life. She is the flaw-less mirror, perfectly reflecting the love of God.

She was prepared for this life in the womb by the Holy Spirit. She was conceived immaculate, the culmination of God's plan for the Birth of His Son. The same Holy Spirit Who swept over the face of creation to draw from it that perfect human response, that *fiat*, through which the Word became flesh, has shaped the destiny of each one of us, preparing us for the work God intends for us to do.

We are, like Mary, though usually less dramatically, asked to give our unconditional yes to that plan—no strings at-tached, no bargain struck. We are simply to wait faithfully upon the Holy Spirit in quietness, fed by prayer and re-flection on the Scriptures and faith strengthened by Holy Communion and the sacrament of Reconciliation.

Mary's vocation is to be the *Theotokos*, "God-bearer." It is from her that God took human nature. She is the Mother of God, and so in the Birth of Jesus she holds up the Savior to the waiting world.

Mary's vocation is our vocation through Baptism. We are also to be God-bearers who hold up the Savior to a waiting world through our lives of faithfulness and obedi-ence. We, too, must say to God, "Let it be to me according to your word" (Luke 1:38). Mary's work was not finished at the Nativity; her Divine Motherhood means far more than that. Her whole life was focused on her Son and directed others toward Him. She lived entirely for Him and so continuously absorbed the Holy Spirit, who penetrated her every thought, word, and action. It became impossible to distinguish what was the prompting of the Spirit and what was the prompting of her own heart.

Mary was so much a part of her Son that she shared in His suffering for the redemption of the world. She was so transformed by grace, so charged with the Holy Spirit that she became the perfectly redeemed human being, the first to be taken up into the glory of Heaven, which is the destiny of all of us.

We have access to the same grace that was given to Mary and to all the saints! We're called to the same vocation as Mary and all the saints were! So, let us allow the grace of the Holy Spirit to grow within us so that we can carry Our Lord, Mary's Son, with us and in us and between us wherever we go and whatever we do.

THE WORD WAS MADE FLESH

Fr. John S. Hogan, 2008

St. Peter's Church, National Shrine of
St. Oliver Plunkett, Drogheda, Ireland

Loreto is a small medieval city, perched atop a small mountain overlooking the Adriatic Sea on the east coast of Italy. If you look up from the plains below, you see a great wall reminiscent of a fortress, a forbidding citadel; in reality, it is a spiritual doorway, a place of meeting. Within the walls is a great basilica and, beneath the dome of the basilica, a marble chapel within which is an ancient house, simple in its construction but resonant with history. This is the house of Nazareth where the Annunciation took place, where it is believed the Holy Family lived and St. Joseph died — the Holy House that was and is a witness to the mystery of the Incarnation.

Loreto is a place where it is easy to pray. The ancient stones of the Holy House seem to speak, like the stones of Jerusalem that Jesus said would cry out in testament to Him. In this House of Mary, you are an honored guest, and her hospitality is the peace and serenity of encounter with God. Words written over the altar in that little house remind you of the significance of this place: "Here the Word was made flesh." We believe in the Incarnation, and yet coming to the place where it happened, one encounters the mystery in a new way. Of course, we do not need to go to Loreto to experience this: We need only reflect on the account of the Annunciation, the Gospel for this Fourth Sunday of Advent, and we can enter into the mystery in the Word of God.

The Holy House of Loreto stands as a sign to the world that the mystery of Christ is real. The story of God's becoming man is not a myth or a legend, not something esoteric or abstract or beyond our comprehension. The House is also a sign of God's invitation for us to enter into the mystery of Christ's life here and now. The mystery of the Incarnation is to be part of our everyday lives, because it was lived in the home of Nazareth and can be lived in every other home, in every other life.

For centuries, the people of Israel waited, hoping that the promised Messiah would come in their lifetime. It is said that every Jewish girl wondered if she would be the one chosen to become his mother. These were not entirely innocent hopes: Many Jews understood the Messiah to be a political and military leader, so the honor of being his mother would have brought with it earthly glory, a vindication of Israel, and the restoration of a downtrodden people. The mother of the Messiah would, without doubt, symbolize these things in her own person. However, who would ever have thought that the Messiah would come in such a quiet, humble way?

Perhaps the House of Nazareth was silent for the few moments following Our Lady's assent, but no doubt Heaven was ecstatic in praise at the Incarnation of the Son of God in the womb of the Virgin, as He took upon Himself the flesh of sinful humanity and transformed it. Who would have ever thought that God would become man and live in our midst? He could have redeemed us from above, but He chose to become one of us, like us in all things but sin, even while being taken for a sinner. This is the mystery of the Incarnation that we celebrate at Christmas and prepare for in Advent.

But after those few moments of glory, it was a return to ordinary daily life for the Mother of God; the world was, as yet, unaware. With the Son of God growing within her, this first Christian disciple began the era of the New Covenant as a missionary, setting out immediately to bring the presence of Christ to one who was in need, her cousin Elizabeth. Full of grace, with the God of love within her, Mary shared that love in her act of service.

In those first moments, hours, and days of the Incarnation, in Mary's service we see that the mystery must take effect in our daily lives, ordinary and humdrum as they may be. As God has become man to live His life with us, He asks us to come to Him and live our lives with Him. The Incarnation is a two-way street: God took flesh so we may come to share in His divinity. Our restoration is not to a previous life, but to a new way of living. This is the heroic way of the saints, the spiritual way that is the greatest adventure of all because it is a journey into the life of God, into His mystery, where we will find the fullness of life. Advent is the time when we prepare for this transformation: Liturgically it is four weeks, but it is really our whole lives, a preparation for the second coming of Christ. This is what our Christian vocation is all about.

The Annunciation was the moment when Mary discovered her vocation, and Jesus Christ revealed His. The mystery of Christ's Incarnation, of His vocation in our midst, leads us to reflect on our own vocation. At the Annunciation, Mary echoed what Jesus would say in the Garden of Gethsemane: "Thy will be done." We are called to make this assent in our lives. God has a plan for us that is firmly situated within His plan for all of humanity; we are to incarnate Christ in the world through our lives. We have the choice to embrace that plan or to reject it, and we can even pick and choose, doing the bits we like and ignoring those we do not. God has given us the gift of free will, and He allows us to decide. Ultimately, though, our true happiness lies in assenting to God's will, in saying yes to His plan in its totality and discerning, through prayer, what we are to do in the circumstances He presents us with.

This can be difficult. Most of the time, it seems that God speaks to us indirectly, but the truth is that He is always communicating with us, and we are not always focused enough to listen. It's usually not obvious, like the angel Clarence in *It's a Wonderful Life*. More often, God asks us simply to turn to listen to Him in prayer.

Pious artists often depict Mary at prayer when Gabriel appears. Whether this reflects a historical reality is less important than that it reflects a spiritual reality: Mary was a woman of profound prayer. When the angel came, she was already tuned in to the voice of the Lord, listening to receive His word. If we wish to discover what God asks us to do at any stage in our lives, we must also be men and women of prayer. And within the context of the relationship of prayer, we will discover who we are and what God offers us as our vocation.

A few years ago, a friend of mine, an artist, was discussing his latest project with me. He wanted to do a series of paintings on the Annunciation, and he had been studying the great masters. As an artist, and one with deep faith, he wanted to present the event in a new way, perhaps revealing a dimension that others had neglected. He told me that he was working on the expression on Mary's face, capturing her awestruck reaction to seeing a heavenly being. I thought about it for a moment and then suggested that he look to the angel: What was the angel's reaction when meeting Mary? After all, it was an encounter between the heavenly being and the greatest creature God had ever made, His own Mother. How did Gabriel look on Mary?

The Gospel of the Annunciation invites us to gaze on Mary and to pray in our hearts the words of the liturgy: How shall I fittingly praise you? "Blessed are you among women," St. Elizabeth declares at the Visitation (Luke 1:42): This is humanity's response. We hear God's response in the acclamation, "How beautiful you are, my beloved, how beautiful you are," from the Song of Songs (1:15), as He has filled her with His grace.

As we gaze on her face, therefore, we see the face of the Lord. In her virtues we see His. As His humanity was formed in her womb, His divinity formed her in holiness. In her graciousness and kindness, we see God's as she imitates the One who made her perfect. No one was ever turned from Mary's door, which the first Christians discovered while she was with them, and in testament the Church has loved her and praised her in every age as Mother of the Church. She is the one who can guide us to Jesus and to our place within the communion of His disciples.

In these Advent days, we not only accompany the generations who were waiting for the Messiah, but we also accompany Mary in the last weeks of her pregnancy as she waited for the fulfillment of the promise made to her and to the Jewish people. Advent is Mary's time, during which she prepares us to receive her Son as she received Him in her womb. She must have contemplated His presence within her, immersed herself in His presence. In these days, we can look at her and allow her to take us by the hand and lead us into the midst of the new life Christ offers us, to discover and to live our heavenly vocation.

We are in her womb also, and she seeks to form us in the image of her Son.

Mary, the faithful one, the Mother of God, invites us today, as we ponder the Annunciation, to follow in her footsteps. At the foot of the Cross we were given into her care: We are hers. If we understand Mary's yes to God as representing that of all men and women, then we can begin to enter into the depths of the Christian life — beginning in that little house where the Word became flesh in her so He could become flesh in us and in our lives.

THE SEVEN BELLS OF ADVENT

Fr. Gerard Skinner, 2010

St. Anthony of Padua Church, Rye, England

Over the last three Sundays, we have set out once again to know the Lord through meditating on the saving mysteries of our redemption as they are presented in the life of the Church. During Advent we have drawn strength from all those holy prophets and patriarchs who longed to see the coming of the Messiah, as we remind ourselves that the God Who dwells with us in the Most Holy Eucharist will come again in glory and power to judge all peoples.

During these days, the Church cries out again and again in ancient verse for Her Lord to come. We proclaim mighty antiphons — the great O Antiphons, addressing the Lord with His exalted titles — that express our yearning for Him.

They are heard during Mass at the Gospel acclamation and frame the Magnificat during Vespers in the seven days preceding Christmas. In centuries past, the bells of the monasteries would ring out while these antiphons were sung as if calling to the very heavens for the Lord to come:

O Wisdom of the Most High! You order all things with gentle power: come and teach us the way of prudence.

O Leader of the house of Israel! You gave the law to Moses on Sinai: come and redeem us with outstretched arm.

O Root of Jesse, who stand as a sign to the nations! Come and deliver us: delay no longer.

O Key of David! You open the gates of the eternal Kingdom: come and lead us out of prison where we sit in darkness.

O Emmanuel, our King and Lawgiver! Come and save us, O Lord our God!

O King of the nations and cornerstone of the Church! Come and save man, whom you formed from the clay of the earth.

O Daystar, splendor of eternal light and sun of justice! Come and enlighten those who sit in darkness and the shadow of death.

Let us hear these seven bells of Advent and heed their call; let us enter once again into the Mystery that we are to celebrate.

As we turn to the readings for this Sunday,[16] we see that the prophet Isaiah once again speaks to us. On each Advent Sunday, he has declared a mighty promise, but none as great and as awesome as the one we hear this week: "Therefore the Lord himself will give you a sign. Behold, a young woman shall conceive and bear a son, and shall call his name Immanuel" (Isa. 7:14). "God with us"! Surely this exceeds all the hopes of Israel! The Eternal Word will become flesh, Isaiah prophesies. And not only will the Virgin conceive and give birth, but she will retain her virginity, a conception and a birth entirely fitting for the Creator.

We hear the fulfillment of this prophecy in today's Gospel: Matthew's account (1:18–24) of the Birth of Christ, which focuses on the coming of an angel to Joseph. At first

[16] Lectionary Cycle A.

glance it seems to be a tragic scene: "Her husband Joseph, being a just man and unwilling to put her to shame, resolved to send her away quietly." A beautiful young woman and a fine man, seemingly made for each other, are about to separate after their marriage rites have commenced? It seems to be too terrible. And indeed it is.

Let us briefly consider the virtues of St. Joseph. He was not perfect, but from his actions throughout the Nativity narrative we know that he was a strong, quiet witness to the Divine Mysteries that he was so privileged to participate in. He knew Mary as the perfect bride, and God did not permit the Blessed Virgin to take for a husband any but the most upright of men. As Pope Paul VI memorably said,

> Saint Joseph is the model of those humble ones that Christianity raises to great destinies, and he is the proof that in order to be good and genuine followers of Christ there is no need of "great things"; it is enough to have the common, simple, human virtues, but they need to be true and authentic.[17]

What Sacred Scripture describes is a wondrous scene of intense and exquisite poignancy. Our Blessed Lady and

[17] Homily on the feast of St. Joseph, 1969.

St. Joseph are in a room by themselves, as the simple carpenter listens to the humble Virgin's story of this Divine Conception. We do not know what words were spoken, yet this moving moment has all the beauty and power of scenes the Gospels flesh out more fully, such as the Visitation. St. Joseph surely felt the Divine Presence before his beloved uttered a word. Indeed, I suspect few words were said, and the silence of awe filled that room.

The words of the saints, though, can enlighten our imaginations. In her *Revelations*, St. Bridget of Sweden attributes these words to Our Lady:

> After I gave my consent to God's messenger, Joseph, seeing my womb enlarged by the power of the Holy Spirit, was exceedingly afraid. It is not that he suspected me of anything untoward but simply that he remembered the words of the prophets when they foretold the birth of the Son of God from a virgin and reckoned himself unworthy of serving such a mother, until the angel in a dream commanded him not to be afraid to serve me with charity.[18]

---

[18] *Revelations*, VII, 25.

The fifteenth-century theologian and mystic Denys the Carthusian reflected:

> There is no doubt that the interior grace, sanctity, and chastity of Mary shone forth wonderfully and powerfully, not only in her face but in the bearing and deportment of her body, so much so that anyone diligently considering her manner of life could not suspect her of fornication or of any other sin.[19]

And the Angelic Doctor, St. Thomas Aquinas, concurred with this understanding of St. Joseph's intentions:

> Joseph had no suspicion of adultery, for he was well aware of Mary's chastity. He had read in Scripture that a virgin would conceive.... He also knew that Mary was descended from David. It was easier, therefore, for him to believe that this had been fulfilled in her than that she had committed fornication. And so, regarding himself as unworthy to live under the same roof with someone of such sanctity, he wanted to put her away privately, as Peter said, "Leave me, Lord, for I am a sinful man."[20]

[19] *Enarratio in evangelium secundum Matthaeum*, I, a. 3.
[20] *Lectura supra Mattaeum*, I, 4.

The silent St. Joseph is preeminently a man of great humility, not a man embarrassed by what the neighbors will say if they find out about this Divine Conception. He is transparently set on serving God whatever the cost, and he gives us a powerful lesson in the virtues of obedience to a well-formed conscience and of listening carefully to the promptings of the Lord.

St. Joseph, like the Blessed Virgin, is highly sensitive to the voice of God given through the angels. He seems to dwell in their presence: There is no sense of shock or surprise that an angel has spoken to him. In this, Joseph gives us another important lesson for our Christian lives.

Every Sunday, we gather together with the saints and the angels at Mass. The church is continually inhabited by God's glorious messengers, adoring Him in the Blessed Sacrament and assisting at the Sacrifice. Most famously we think of Michael, the leader of the warriors of God, and Gabriel, the strength of God, and Raphael, the healing of God. And we should regularly celebrate and pray to those angels that God has given us as guardians, who guide us on our pilgrim journeys to their home above.

Scripture is full of references to such guides. Abraham, when sending his steward to seek a wife for Isaac, says, "The LORD ... will send his angel with you and prosper your way" (Gen. 24:40). In the book of Exodus, God tells His people, "Behold, I send an angel before you, to guard you on the way and to bring you to the place which I have prepared. Give heed to him and hearken to his voice" (Exod. 23:20–21). Later in the Old Testament, the psalmist prays, "The angel of the LORD encamps around those who fear him, and delivers them" (Ps. 34:7). And Christ Himself, Whose whole earthly ministry was surrounded by the ministrations of the angels, said: "See that you do not despise one of these little ones; for I tell you that in heaven their angels always behold the face of my Father who is in heaven" (Matt. 18:10).

We rarely sense the presence of the angels, but perhaps it's at Christmas that we are most aware of them. We sing of them in our hymns and see them on our greeting cards and place them in our Nativity scenes and on our Christmas trees.

Before I went to seminary, I was an organ scholar at Westminster Cathedral in London. It is a vast Byzantine-style building with a dark, cavernous ceiling; when you are there at night, it's almost as if the sky is opened to you. I will never forget my first Christmas Day there, in the evening, when the cathedral was closed, dark, and silent. It was an ecstatic experience. The place was still, yet somehow trembling with the excitement of the Nativity. There was immense life there, and the atmosphere was electric: It seemed that the angels were dancing, celebrating the Birth of the Lord.

CHRISTMAS

THE CRIB AND THE CROSS

Archbishop Michael Neary, 2004

Our Lady's Shrine, Knock, County Mayo, Ireland

Christmas is history: a little Child in a Crib. But it is also mystery: God with us.

The story of the Birth of Jesus was not the first part of the Gospel to be written down: It was recorded in light of the Death and Resurrection of Christ. You might say that the story of the Birth and Infancy of Jesus is written with Death and Resurrection ink. The story is colored by the early Christian experience of preaching the gospel—which, like Jesus Himself, was received by pagans but rejected by the Jews—and so these insights that emanated from the Death and Resurrection found their way into the story of the Birth and Infancy.

At His Death, Jesus was rejected by His own but acknowledged by the centurion on behalf of the pagan world. At His Birth, Jesus is rejected by Herod and Jerusalem but accepted by the Magi, also representing the pagan world. St. Matthew and St. Luke give not merely a chronicle of cold facts but also an interpretation — their own theological reflections on the events. As a result, the story of the Nativity provides a vantage point for reading the whole story of Jesus Christ. We are given a special insight that provides us with more information than even those who interacted with Jesus during His ministry.

The events surrounding the Birth of Jesus point us to the past and the future. On the one hand, they look to the past, where we see the hopes and longings of the Old Testament fulfilled. At the same time, the Nativity narrative looks to the future, heralding what will take place in Jesus' public ministry. For example, at His Birth, Jesus was wrapped in swaddling clothes and laid in a manger. At His Death, He was wrapped in a burial cloth and laid in a rock-hewn tomb by Joseph of Arimathea.

The manger and the swaddling clothes also, of course, demonstrate the poverty into which Jesus was born. But St. Luke insists that in this sign of powerlessness, people will recognize the Savior of the world: "And this will be a sign for you: you will find a babe wrapped in swaddling cloths and lying in a manger" (Luke 2:12). This may be an illusion to King Solomon, son of David, who claimed to be the royal child since he, like all kings, had been wrapped in swaddling cloths. Every time a descendant of David ascended the throne, it was hoped that this king would prove to be the ideal king, the Messiah. St. Luke is therefore presenting Jesus as Son of God and true king.

The church that sits at the traditional location of Christ's Birth has a very unusual feature: The door of entry is very low, so low that one has to stoop in order to enter. When we think of Christmas and the Incarnation, we are really reflecting on the feast of the stooping down of God, His condescension. Our planet is but a tiny speck among the stars of the universe, and the Hand that spun the stars shivered in the cold of earth in Bethlehem. That was the beginning of the stooping down of God, and it continued until the day He allowed Himself to be nailed to a Cross — and it continues to this day in the form of the Eucharist.

When He arrived in Bethlehem, He did so very gently. Everything in Bethlehem suggests gentleness. Mary and Joseph accepted gently being turned away at the inn. The shepherds listened to the message of the angels and gently made their way to Bethlehem to find the Child and His Mother. The Magi gently received the answer of the jealous Herod and continued their journey from Jerusalem to Bethlehem until they found the manger. There would be so much more peace in our lives if we knew how to be truly gentle with ourselves and with others. When the Infant of Bethlehem grew to manhood, He asked His followers to learn from Him so that they would be gentle and humble of heart.

An infant is the least threatening of all humans. A newborn is helpless, his simple and straightforward language — that is, his cry — is that of dependence and humility. The language of God at Christmas is the language of love, the language of humility and simplicity. Our call, as followers of Jesus Christ, is to learn that language, not only at Christmas, but throughout the year. The season brings to the surface social attitudes that may be less apparent at other time. We become more aware of the polarization in our culture as Christmas brings out the opposites: generosity and greed, gentleness and violence, kindness and coarseness, patience and bullying.

If we reflect on some of the characters at the first Christmas, we should not be surprised. The all-powerful Creator was now present in the most unlikely of places, as a Baby in a Bethlehem manger. Innocence had come to dwell in what was part of the sophisticated Roman Empire. There was goodness and fidelity in the persons of Mary and Joseph but, just as is the case so often in our world today, they were marginalized. They did not have access to the levers of economic and political power. They trusted in God in order that He would take up their cause. They represented a hope that refused to die.

Two thousand years later, we are invited to be open to the Lord and to respond to the signs and opportunities He gives us. We are invited to undertake the mystical journey to Bethlehem, to the place where God came to us. It is a place of mystery and wonder far removed from the ordinary world in which we live.

This Christmas, let us examine ourselves and our situations and find where there is pain that points to our need for a Savior. In a busy world, there is a danger that we may not notice those areas of need, or that we may misinterpret them and fail to recognize their true source. We find ourselves caught so frequently between the pull of conscience and that of culture. It is difficult for generosity and goodness to survive in a world dominated by competitiveness, in a culture where productivity is considered more valuable than principles or people. The goodness that is in each one of us and that manifests itself particularly at Christmastime needs to be nurtured throughout the year.

Where there is goodness, there is hope. Hope involves looking life in the face and finding God at the very center. There are two basic elements in hope: first, the courage to face reality as it is; second, an awareness of God's presence, a presence that sustains us and gives us strength. Christmas is a time when we become acutely aware of the presence and the closeness of God. We recognize that Jesus takes us beyond the narrow view of our culture, beyond the grasping greed and the constant busyness, as He comes to nourish the good that is in us and to enable that good to be expressed.

This time of year, many of us will be undertaking journeys home, or visiting family and friends. But each of us also needs to journey back to Bethlehem. There, we will remember our more fundamental journey: where we've come from, where we find ourselves right now, and where we hope to go. This Christmas should enable us to see where we are in that journey and to look forward to where we want to go, including understanding what part Christ plays in this journey and what our true destiny and purpose is meant to be.

Looking at this journey, we need to find hope, and we need to consider how that hope determines the way we live the destiny we have in mind—the destiny we hope for. Hope is life-giving. Hope thrives on promises, and this Christmas, let us remember that God has kept His promise, and therefore there is hope for each one of us. We can and must be people of irrepressible hope.

THE DAY OF OUR REDEMPTION

Bishop Alan Hopes, 2005

St. Etheldreda Church, Ely Place, London, England

Enveloped in silence and surrounded by night in a foreign town, wrapped in poverty and cloaked in fragility, God begins His pilgrimage as man. He Who is uncreated, He Who is the Eternal, He Who is the Force and Power behind the universe, He Who our finite minds cannot comprehend: This Infinite Being became a human being. God becomes man, so that man can become part of His life. No longer is the Divine remote and unapproachable. No longer is He removed and shrouded in mystery. But God is here with man, His fellow traveler. He is Emmanuel, "God with us."

So much has gone into the making of man. He is the crown of God's creation, endowed with that most terrible and wonderful of all gifts, freedom. We've hardly begun to understand the complexity of human minds, and the capabilities of human potential. And still men and women cry and starve and fight and die of loneliness and are frightened and fragile and broken. And it is in man's fragility and brokenness and poverty that God Himself joins us.

And so the sign that is given to us today is man's own poverty. Says St. Paul, as he writes of the Incarnation, "For you know the grace of our Lord Jesus Christ, that though he was rich, yet for your sake he became poor, so that by his poverty you might become rich" (2 Cor. 8:9). The recognition of our poverty is the beginning of rediscovering our wholeness. Once we let the God of the poor join us on our pilgrim way, then, through the sacraments, He binds our wounds and heals our sorrows and makes us whole again. Love of any sort always enriches and transforms; it can make giants out of pygmies.

The first to recognize this heavenly sign were the simple shepherds, in whose lives the sign of poverty must have resonated. Leaving everything, they came to Mary's knee to find what their restless hearts had always sought. Pope St. Leo the Great, in one of his Christmas homilies in the fifth century, had this to say:

O Christian, be aware of your nobility. It is God's Own Nature that you share. Do not then by ignoble fall, fall back into your former basis. Think of the Head, think of the Body of which you are a member. Record that you have been rescued from the power of darkness and have been transferred to the Light of God, the Kingdom of God. Through the Sacrament of Baptism you have been made a Temple of the Holy Spirit. Do not by evil deeds drive so great an Indweller away from you, submitting yourself once more to the slavery of the devil, for you were bought at the price of Christ's Blood.

St. Leo reminds us of just how beautiful and lovely and noble our human nature can be—when it is in tune with the Creator. When it is not, we see the dark side of human nature, the evil that we are capable of. Our world is still full of the threat of conflict, of violence, of contempt for human dignity and human life. Even Bethlehem, where the Prince of Peace was born, is now a symbol of division and conflict.

St. Leo also reminds us that the Incarnation of Our Lord—His coming to share in our human nature—comes with a price. Yes, God comes into the messiness and fragility and suffering of humanity to live out the way of love — but that love led Jesus Christ to the Cross.

We began our journey to this day four weeks ago. Through those weeks we've been helped in our preparation by the prophet Isaiah, who foretold the coming of Jesus; by John the Baptist, who proclaimed Him when He came; and, of course, by Mary, who brought forth the Savior into our world. The story of our salvation is one continuous, seamless story. It begins with Creation and culminates in the Birth, Life, Death, and Resurrection of Our Lord.

In the Gospel reading for Christmas Day (John 1:1–5, 9–14), St. John leads us into this great mystery of our faith:

In the beginning was the Word, and the Word was with God, and the Word was God. He was in the beginning with God; all things were made through him, and without him was not anything made that was made. In him was life, and the life was the light of men. The light shines in the darkness, and the darkness has not overcome it.

The true light that enlightens every man was coming into the world. He was in the world, and the world was made through him, yet the world knew him not. He came to his own home, and his own people received him not. But to all who received him, who believed in his name, he gave power to become children of God; who were born, not of blood nor of the will of the flesh nor of the will of man, but of God. And the Word became flesh and dwelt among us, full of grace and truth.

From the beginning, when the Spirit of God hovered over the formless void of nonbeing, there was only darkness and silence. Then, "Let there be Light!" God's Holy Majesty, in compassion and strength, drew back the veil of His glory and allowed the Light to explode into the dark, and live matter to form and develop. Darkness became the symbol of death and misery, of the path of sin and nonbeing, of oblivion and loss. Light became the symbol of God's presence and majesty, the place of peace and purpose and love, the way of life, renewed in holiness.

This image of light appears throughout Scripture in relation to the story of salvation. The old Jewish Law was given by divine intervention and was, as the psalmist says, "a lamp to my feet and a light to my path" (Ps. 119:105). Isaiah, together with the other prophets, came looking to the horizon for the Messiah, Who would be "a light for revelation to the Gentiles, and for glory to thy people

Israel" (Luke 2:32). Then John the Baptist came, and the light of faith began to flame. John was "a burning and shining lamp" that had to be lit (John 5:35), a flame fed by blood in preparation for the coming of the True Light, the Light that no darkness can ever overpower.

And so, in the silence of deep mystery and under the pale light of the strange star, the Light of the World descended and took human form, born of a pure Virgin. The day of our redemption dawned. The reign of shadows was over. The brilliant Light of God's presence flooded into history. And the Light was held in the frail arms of humanity. She who brought the Light into the world gathered Him to herself. All others share in fragments and splinters of the Light; Mary shared in its totality, then and now. Her memory is the memory of the Church, and through the waters of Baptism and under the light of the Easter candle, we are given this memory, the living memory of the whole Christ.

For thirty years, the Light lived hidden in Mary's love and care—and then burst into a flame that consumes all darkness. At first, His disciples were skeptical and lighthearted, joking, "Can anything good come out of Nazareth?" (John 1:46). The Light waited and pondered in love and in silence. Then the hesitation faded, and they were

His, and He was theirs. In Him, they began to glimpse the working of God Himself, and the Light of God's presence touched their hearts. They believed. "Lord, to whom shall we go? You have the words of eternal life" (John 6:68).

Good Friday was the end, the last day of all that they had ever hoped or lived for. It was dense and obscure and dark. It was the last day of history. It was the last day of their lives because He, their Light, had been taken from them. The darkness of human hatred and evil and sin seemed to have won. The Light was extinguished.

And that is why they ran to the tomb on Easter. It was unbelievable! It was a complete reversal of all that had seemed to be. And suddenly, light and love and life and hope flooded back into their lives. Darkness did not, and does not, have the final say. The Light had returned, never again to leave them. His first words are those of peace, "Peace be with you," and they were young again (John 20:19). And ever since that moment, the victory of the Lord Jesus Christ has burned in the hearts of men and women everywhere, making them young again in hope and love.

From that incredible life, which emerged in Bethlehem, a flame was lit that has burned through the centuries — and that we have within us: His sacred Presence in the Eucharist of His Body and Blood.

Yes, there is darkness in our world in the form of war and terrorism; in the form of hunger, homelessness, and poverty; in the form of selfishness and greed. But there is no darkness anywhere that can extinguish this Light, which is Our Lord Jesus Christ, the King of Kings and Lord of Lords, victorious and triumphant, whose love and grace illuminates all of creation. It is Our Lord Jesus Christ, in Whose presence is our true home, for Whose sake we were born, and in Whose love is our eternal destiny.

About the Authors

Fr. Richard Biggerstaff

Fr. Richard Biggerstaff is a priest of the Diocese of Arundel and Brighton.

Fr. Ronald Creighton-Job

Fr. Ronald Creighton-Jobe, C.O., is a priest of the London Oratory. He entered the novitiate in 1968, after earning an honors degree in English literature at King's College, London. He continued his studies, earning a B.D. in theology at Heythrop College, and was ordained a priest in 1973.

Fr. Stewart Foster

Fr. Stewart Foster is archivist of the Diocese of Brentwood (England) and diocesan coordinator for Mass in the Extraordinary Form. A graduate of Middlesex, London, and Hull Universities, he holds a doctorate in the history of Catholic education. He is the author of several books and many articles on historical and theological topics, a former editor of *Catholic Archives*, and currently a council member of the Catholic Record Society.

Fr. Shane Gallagher

Fr. Shane Gallagher felt called to the priesthood while teaching high school. He entered St. Patrick's Seminary in Maynooth in 2002 and, after four years of study, was sent to the Irish College in Rome, where he finished his studies at the Angelicum University and received a licenciate in sacred theology (STL). He was ordained a priest for the Diocese of Raphoe in Ireland in 2008 and serves as a full-time hospital chaplain in that diocese.

About the Authors

Fr. John S. Hogan

Fr. John S. Hogan is a priest of the Diocese of Meath, Ireland, and a Secular Order Discalced Carmelite. Author and co-host of the EWTN series *Forgotten Heritage*, he has worked as a parish priest, chaplain, teacher, and retreat director. He is the founder of the Fraternity of St. Genesius, an association that supports and prays for those involved in the theatrical and cinematic arts.

Bishop Alan Hopes

The Right Reverend Alan Hopes, B.D., A.K.C., studied theology at King's College, London, and then attended Warminster Theological College before receiving Anglican Orders in 1968. He was later received into full communion with the Catholic Church and was ordained a priest in 1995. In 2003, Pope Benedict XVI appointed him auxiliary bishop of Westminster, and in 2013, Pope Francis appointed him the fourth bishop of East Anglia, England. He is chair of the Committee for Liturgy and is a member of the Bishops' Conference Department of Christian Life and Worship.

Fr. Pat Lombard

Fr. Pat Lombard is a priest of the Diocese of Elphin, Ireland.

Archbishop Michael Neary

Archbishop Michael Neary studied for the priesthood at St. Patrick's College, Maynooth, County Kildare, Ireland. He was ordained in the Cathedral of the Assumption, Tuam, in 1971. Archbishop Neary undertook postgraduate studies in theology and was awarded a doctor of divinity degree in Maynooth in 1975. After three years of ministering in the diocese, he studied Sacred Scripture in Rome and was awarded the L.S.S. in 1981. From 1982 until his appointment as auxiliary bishop of Tuam in 1992, he taught at the National Seminary in Maynooth. Since 1995, he has been Archbishop of Tuam.

Fr. Gerard Skinner

Fr. Gerard Skinner studied at the Royal Academy of Music in London and the Venerable English College in Rome. A priest of the Archdiocese of Westminster, England, he has written, edited, or contributed to a number of books, including *Newman the Priest: A Father of Souls*, *The Pallium: A Brief Guide to Its History and Significance*, and *Father Ignatius Spencer: English Noble and Christian Saint.*

Fr. Vincent Twomey

D. Vincent Twomey is a Divine Word Missionary priest. After earning his doctorate under the supervision of Professor Joseph Ratzinger (the future Pope Benedict XVI) at the University of Regensburg, he taught dogmatic theology at Holy Spirit Regional Seminary, Papua New Guinea, and at the SVD Faculty of Theology at St. Gabriel's, Mödling, Austria, before his appointments as lecturer in moral theology and then as professor at the Pontifical University, Maynooth, Ireland. He was appointed visiting professor at the Dominican University of Fribourg, Switzerland, and visiting scholar at Seton Hall University, New Jersey. He has been featured prominently in public discourse in Ireland and has published extensively.